Dare to Imagine

18 Principles for Finding Peace, Happiness, and True Success

A True Story of Hope and Love,
Divinely Inspired

BLAKE SINCLAIR

Dare to Imagine:
18 Principles for Finding Peace, Happiness, and True Success
Copyright © 2014 by Blake Sinclair

ISBN: 978-1494994051 (pbk)

Edited by Dana Leipold
www.danaleipold.com

Cover design by Airi Beltran
www.airibeltran.com

eBook formatting by Maureen Cutajar
www.gopublished.com

Important Note to Readers:
The intent of the author is to offer information on the author's own spiritual evolution and awakening with the hope of motivating readers to release their hidden and latent potential for living a more productive, happy, and peaceful life. The author is not a licensed physician and does not offer medical advice. Any lifestyle change with regard to health needs to be addressed with the reader's physician or appropriate health care provider.

This book is dedicated to my wife and children. You have all taught me how to live, love and laugh. May you always remember that you are a spark of light from God and that the answers of the great mysteries of the universe are not so far away but within yourself.

TABLE OF CONTENTS

INTRODUCTION

When people think of San Francisco, they think of Chinatown, Fisherman's Wharf, cable cars, or the Golden Gate Bridge. They think of the great shopping, diverse cuisines and exceptional sightseeing. Others think of it as a romantic city by the bay.

When I think of San Francisco, I recall bittersweet memories of an ordinary kid who was born happy but was thrown into a world full of fear and uncertainty. It seemed that most of my life I was surrounded by negative people: my family, my friends, my teachers, classmates, co-workers, and even those from my Chinese culture. My future seemed so bleak and hopeless. My only hope was to try to escape reality by any and all means possible. At 21 years old, I felt so alone. I was at the lowest point in my life. I tried calling my friends but they were all too busy to talk and I didn't want to bother anyone. I ended up leaving a suicide note for my parents. It didn't take long until my mother and sister discovered my note. They rushed over to me to give me support, and that little bit of love created my first glimmer of hope in my life.

That day prompted my start for the search for the meaning in life. I had many questions but no answers I wasn't sure what to do, but knew I wasn't happy, where my life was, and that I required a change. I decided to work hard and do well in school and make something of myself. I worked hard to achieve the American dream: getting a job, a family, and material things because I thought they would bring me happiness. They only brought me stress, anxiety, and, despair. I became depressed by all the challenges of life and the lack of love wherever I went. I began experiencing physical and emotional sicknesses.

I sought help through the medical system, and thought that was where I would find healing. Medicine did wonders to get rid of my physical symptoms. My doctors would arm me with arsenals of medicine to keep depression and anxiety at bay. However, they would always come back to haunt me. I would get stronger medicine but then sometimes I would have adverse side effects. I never felt completely happy or peaceful. I was always at war with my emotions and inner demons.

I needed something more so I searched for happiness through alternative therapies technique like Hypnosis and NeiGong. These techniques all helped me in achieving greater peace and happiness but my soul still thirsted for something else. I went to traditional talk therapy and even did cognitive behavioral therapy from very caring and loving marriage and family therapists (MFTs). These techniques helped me to become aware of my thought patterns and behavior and how by changing them I could gain greater peace and harmony in my life.

Finally, I began a spiritual journey that helped me make a final, life-changing transformation. I discovered that the love I had sought for so long from my parents, friends, and coworkers was, and has always been, inside of me. I became more compassionate, forgiving, loving, and grateful for all the blessings in my life. I chose to turn away from negative ways of thinking and behaving. I learned to share and give of myself. The more I served and gave, the more I was fulfilled. The ultimate lesson was to receive the true and unconditional love of God and share that love to all of God's creation and people.

When I was a teenager, my friend's grandfather gave me the book, *Les Miserables* by Victor Hugo. He spoke with very limited English but insisted that I read it. To my surprise, I became so engrossed in the book that I completely lost myself in the story. There are so many reasons why I love this story but the evolution of the character Jean Val Jean represents to me, the journey some of us choose to take in finding real peace, happiness, and success. But what sparked this journey was the unconditional love he felt from the bishop who took him in, when no one else would, and stood up for him even when he tried to steal the silver from his residence. It was that moment that he was transformed. Just as I was when I felt the Divine unconditional love when I was in the presence of her holiness, Mata Amritanandamayi (Amma). This book is the story of my journey through the valley of darkness as a young child living in the abyss of hate, anger, and fear—one many of us have had to be faced with through no choice of our own.

Most of us are not born with silver spoons in our mouths. Many of us are born into dysfunctional families, unhealthy environments, and a world of uncertainty. Fortunately, we have two things we can rely on to pull us out of the valley of darkness: choice and Divine, unconditional love. We can choose to see that there is a Divine, unconditional love just waiting for us to reach out and take it. When we do discover it and surrender ourselves to it, we find the true riches within our hearts and find true happiness and success. We do not have to accept the horrible situations we have been born into. We can get out of any situation as long as we are willing, determined, and able to imagine a better life. I know you can because I have done it. I'm here to tell you that you can do it too. Dare to imagine and you will be amazed at where life will take you. My intention in writing this book is to help you on your journey to reclaim your life by manifesting the true and Divine person you really are.

I still live in the San Francisco Bay area, but now those years of fear and uncertainty have been replaced with something deeper: peace, compassion, forgiveness and

Divine, unconditional love. Now I see the beauty in San Francisco, in all people, and in everything in life.

You can too, my friend.

Namaste!

PART I

What Is

*"The season of failure is the best time
for sowing the seeds of success."*
—Paramahansa Yogananda

CHAPTER 1

Born Into Dysfunction

When I was about three years old, I was playing on my mother's bed with my blue toy car busy having fun. Then my simple world was turned upside down. My mother and father were arguing outside of the room but eventually came in where I was playing. I sat there wide-eyed witnessing a violent physical and verbal altercation between the two people I loved so much. My father raised a chair over his head and hit my mother with it. My mother screamed in defense. I knew what my father was doing was wrong but I did not know what to do. However, I did know that my home was no longer a safe haven.

Things seemed to get worse between my mother and father for many years to follow. I would often wake up in the middle of the night and hear my father shouting at my mother. He sounded like a monster to me. She would scream back in her high-pitched voice. It felt like living in a war zone. Once a police officer had to come to our home and intervene. I was so scared that I covered myself with the blanket to try and muffle the nightmare, which seemed to last for an eternity. A few times my father would barge into my room and just rant on, spewing his rage at me. I used to pray, *God, please deliver me from this nightmare. Blake wake up, this is not real.*

My brother, sister, and I never said anything or got involved because my father was extremely intimidating. He was a sergeant in the army and was as tough as nails. He had been known to chase real gangsters who tried to confront him. My father was a volatile person and did not have any control of his emotions. We were terrified of him. He was a workaholic and would come home late a lot. He had a regular day job as a machinist foreman for an automotive battery tooling company, down in Santa Clara County. When he was finished with work, he would then manage the apartments that his parents had owned. He would do all the repairs and sometimes asked me to assist him. I was always nervous about helping him because I never knew what to expect from him. I used to daydream a lot to escape the painful reality of my home life.

One time, I was helping my father and my job was to hold the flashlight while he did the repair. I think I was about 12 years old. He ended up yelling because I was holding the flashlight wrong, but I was probably daydreaming. His loud voice was so powerful, beating me down for how stupid I was for not holding the flashlight right. I began to think that maybe I was an idiot for not being able to do such a simple task. Other times he would lecture me then go on and on about my stupidity when I was helping him on his repair jobs. Once I broke down because I couldn't handle what he was saying to me. I felt dizzy like I was going to throw up. When I told my father about my nausea, he looked at me with disgust and contempt. His look pierced through me and I couldn't even throw up. Maybe I was a useless and lousy son.

My mother was not as severe as my father but she had her moments. She would often get impatient with me and transform from a loving and caring mother to the most negative person I could imagine. She would spew out hurtful words and sentences in her Taishanese dialect that were like daggers and swords wounding my heart. Once she tried to teach me to write Chinese calligraphy with an ink brush when I was eight years old. For a while, she tried to work with me but when I messed up, she would end up yelling, "No! No! No!" She seized my hand and forced me to write the correct way and that made me become passive which made her even more furious. She would yell at me in Chinese and accuse me of being deaf because I would start to tune out her and not listen to her. I noticed that she would talk about her friend's kids being so smart and how they were able to do this and that. I tried my best to please her but no matter how hard I tried, I was never good enough. She would always tell me how someone else was better. I wondered if she did that to try and make me work harder but these comments only made me feel more insecure and inadequate.

Watching the *Brady Bunch* on television made me wish for a different family. I would imagine that I was in every episode with a mother and father I could confide in and with whom I felt safe and loved. It made me so sad that I was trapped in a nightmare hoping I could wake up to a loving family one day. I wished I could just do something right for once. I was useless, especially to my family. I felt it was my fault that I was not worthy of love because I was born different and stupid. If I had been smarter my parents would have been pleased and happy with me. Perhaps the world outside my family would be more promising?

Although I attended decent schools, I never felt worthy of them. I developed anxiety attacks whenever I was in a situation where people were watching me do something. The angry eyes of my father and mother haunted me in these situations. I would sweat, lose focus, and freeze up. This only made things worse for me in school. Daydreaming would help me escape my negative reality, but in turn doing so caused me to have greater challenges in school I had difficulty focusing on subject matters that proved too difficult like chemistry and mathematics.

Back in the 60's, most Chinese kids who lived in San Francisco were expected to attend Chinese language school, and I was no exception. The school is not really designed well for what the immigrants would call us, *ABCs* (which means American Born Chinese) or *jook sing* (which means hollow bamboo or dumb). The teachers who taught the class were all immigrants who either had limited English or did not speak it all. I hated Chinese school because I wasn't good at it, especially when I got to higher levels and could not comprehend some of the deeper subjects. I remember one particular teacher I had in third grade actually asked me in front of other students, "Why are you so stupid?" Not only was I speechless and shocked but embarrassed beyond belief. I didn't know what to say so I just shrugged my shoulders. I wanted to run away and cry but I didn't for fear of being seen as weak. Yet deep down inside myself I accepted his comment, believing what he said as being the truth. If my parents and my teacher thought I was stupid maybe I really was condemned to be an idiot for the rest of my life.

Rejection from my family and school was difficult to bear but then I began feeling it from other Chinese people. I was called jook sing by some, always resenting it. Yet within myself I had no respect for those who said it, because somewhere inside I knew that it was not true. One thing I noticed is that if my immigrant friends did not know the truth about where I was from, life was easier. So I began lying about where I was from just to be accepted. If I told them I was from Hong Kong, I was instantly accepted to any group. I tried so hard to be accepted that I even picked up my immigrant friend's accent too. I studied Gung Fu for several years with a renowned martial art instructor in San Francisco. Even he treated me with discrimination despite how well I was doing. He once told a prospective Chinese student (who was from Hong Kong) in Chinese how I didn't know anything because I was a *jook sing*. Unbeknownst to him, I understood everything he said. It didn't matter how hard I worked or how good I was, I was branded inferior just by my place of birth.

In many Asian cultures, a person with fair skin is considered beautiful. In fact, in China there is a saying that goes, *may yun ywe yook*, which translates into English as a beautiful person is likened to be the beauty of a jade. Those with darker skin are seen as lower class and treated like dirt. In Western culture, those who have time and money have tan skin. When I was young, my skin was quite fair but as I started to align myself more with my westernized friends, I tanned to become darker because it was the in thing. I was so thirsty for acceptance that making my skin darker offered me some acceptance by my Western friends.

Despite these friends, my self-hatred grew and took root. I grew angry with myself and wished that I had never been born. I wasn't good enough for my family, in school, and for my own race. I lived in a very lonely world.

Many of us are born into dysfunctional families, bad circumstances, or are faced with insurmountable challenges. An infant has done nothing to deserve anger directed at it by parents dealing with their own pain and turmoil. A child does nothing to deserve blatant discrimination because of how he looks or where he was born. All of this stress and trauma can have a lasting effect that lingers on into adulthood. These situations become the foundation that we build our fragile sense of self upon. Such dysfunctional realities often leave us with scars in our mental and feeling bodies; scars that left unhealed, build within us as we journey into adulthood

CHAPTER 2

Too Much Negativity Can Push Us to the Edge

*D*espite the chaos in my early childhood years, there was one person who brought light and hope in my life: my grandmother. She moved in to live with us when I was young. My grandmother acted as a buffer between my parents and I. Whenever my father would become volatile and go ballistic at me, my grandmother would come to my defense. I was always amazed at how my grandmother was so brave and fearless when she stood up to my father who was so scary and menacing. I can only surmise that she loved us so much that her love overcame any fear of my father. She actually stood up and postured herself erect and in a defensive position towards him when he came at me. I believed that if my father attempted to hit me, she would not have allowed that to happen. I could not comprehend how someone so simple, humble, and frail could have so much power and might.

I had many tender moments with my grandmother. She was always a very giving and selfless person. My grandmother would always share her food or drink with me regardless how little she had. It was always about us and not about her. Sometimes, she would methodically peel an orange or skin an apple then when I thought she would eat it, she would quickly hand it to me. Other times she would make me my special and favorite food, rice crust soup, rice balls, and Chinese dumplings. My grandmother was an amazing cook. She would never ask me if I wanted any food. She somehow knew I needed it and wanted it. She somehow knew it would make me feel happy and safe. Also, perhaps the drool from my mouth and the hunger look on my face was a dead giveaway. All joking aside, I took everything from her because I believed everything she gave was good.

We used to play this game during church service. My grandmother would open her hands and I would put my finger in her hand and like a Venus fly trap, she would try to catch it. Often I would escape her trap but there would be times when she would catch me off guard and snatch my finger. I would yell out in the middle of the sermon and we would both laugh while other parishioners would turn around and glare at us. My grandmother read the Bible daily, prayed, and went to church every Sunday. I admired her commitment to her faith. She taught me how to love and give. My grandmother always loved me even when I was being a brat. My grandmother was truly a mother figure in my life. In fact, I once made a speech on Mother's Day about my grandmother being like a mother to me.

My grandmother died in 1984 when I was about 20 years old. I was at home getting ready for school that horrible day but noticed how my mom was extremely distraught as she was pacing back and forth mumbling something. When I asked her what was wrong, she blurted out in Chinese that grandmother had died. I was in complete disbelief. Those words ripped apart my heart. I had never lost anyone that I had loved and this was an extremely painful experience. I quickly rushed over to my grandmother's room and saw her listless body. Her right leg was dangling off the bed as if she was going to get up. I put my hand on her hands and they were cold, dull, and lifeless. I don't know why but I tried to resuscitate her by pounding on her chest and breathing into her mouth like I had seen people do on television. But she was gone.

Within a short time, the coroner came and put her body in a case and took her away. It was such a dismal and empty feeling I felt inside. I was still in so much shock that I couldn't even cry. In fact, it took me over a decade to truly get over her death. I had many nightmares seeing my grandmother and waking up crying profusely because I missed her so much. I refused to accept the fact that she died. Why couldn't I save her? I thought that it must have been my fault that she died. We held the funeral a week later at a local mortuary in Chinatown. It was small and simple. Despite the pastor giving an uplifting eulogy, I had fallen into a state of despair.

After this devastating loss, I expected strong support from our church since we had been loyal parishioners for over a decade but only a small number of people showed their support, and even less showed support from my fellowship group. It was like throwing salt into an open wound. I had gone to all the church events, attended church fellowship every Saturday and Sunday school every week. I volunteered to tell stories to children in Sunday school. I was even a part of choir and a singing group. What did I do wrong? Where were all my fellow brothers and sisters in Christ? We sang, played, and dined together. We opened our hearts to one another and even though I was part of this group, I was alone in my moment of despair.

My protective shield had been stripped away from me. No longer did I have the unconditional love I desperately wanted and needed. My world thrust into chaos and torment again. I would wake up crying thinking about my grandmother. The pain of losing her was greater than anything I had ever felt in my life. I could not understand why God took her away from us. She was my mother figure, angel, and guardian. Why had she been taken from me? My despair at losing her was unbearable. My grandmother, sister, and I were devout with our faith. Why did God allow this to happen? Does God even care about my sister and I? Why couldn't God save her? Then I was angry with God. Was he so busy or was I so insignificant that he did not heed my prayers? Was there a God?

Soon after my grandmother died, I learned that my father was still having an affair. I had heard rumors years before this that he was unfaithful to my mother but I thought he had stopped all this nonsense. I was coping with my grandmother's death as best as I could but my father's ongoing infidelity caused me to feel an enormous amount of shame. I blamed myself for the affair because I wasn't good enough. He seemed to treat the children of his mistress like they were his own children but better. He was nice to them and bought them things. When I was 16, I got my first car from my father. I didn't drive it much because I was nervous about being a new driver. As I was walking home one day I saw my father in *my* car with another family. It was one thing for him to be having a relationship on the side, but it was a big blow when he used what he purchased for me for his own folly. I felt so betrayed. Eventually I repressed those memories thinking it would all go away but unfortunately it never did.

I had lost the source of love in my life, lost my faith in God, and lost hope for my family. I was a loser and my parents, teacher, friends, and those from my Chinese culture seemed to validate it with everything they did or said. My parents basically taught me that I was unworthy. The people in my own culture couldn't accept me and treated me with discrimination. I never would forget that one teacher who asked me why I was so stupid. I had trouble making friends due to my issues with interpersonal skills. I had trouble in school due to my poor attention span and motivation. I felt I was not worthy of love when my church brothers and sisters in Christ did not show up at my grandmother's funeral. All these issues clogged up my mind into a blanket of darkness. What was there to live for? There was no reason. I felt I had no place in this world. I could not bear it anymore. I finally went through a meltdown process and left a suicide note at my parents place in Chinatown.

My parents had purchased a new property in Golden Gate Heights in the 80s and I drove there to escape the pain. My brother was home but I couldn't talk to him. I went upstairs and stared out at the dark and lonely night. It was a long drop from the third floor down to the ground since the house was built on a steep hill. I visualized hurling myself over the balcony and falling to my death. Dying seemed to be the only option that would end the pain but I was also apprehensive because I was afraid of the unknown so I laid on the floor in a fetal position. I cried as the pain swelled up in my heart, which burned away all hope. If I was dead I thought the world would be a better place because I felt that my life had no meaning and no purpose.

As I sank to the bottom of an ocean of despair, I heard the garage door opening downstairs. Then I heard mumbling and footsteps coming up the stairs. I saw my mother's tear-stained face as I laid on the floor in a stupor. She looked so sad as she knelt down and embraced me in her arms. It was the first time she showed me that kind of compassion. My sister stood next to her, also crying in anguish to see me in this state. Slowly I came out of my stupor, confused almost like someone had shined a bright light into my eyes after I had been in darkness for a long time. I thought to myself, *"It is possible that a reject like me can find a reason to live?"* Their love elevated me from the deep depth of my sorrow and revived me. As I came back to reality, the pain poured out of me in a waterfall of tears, out my eyes, down my cheek and neck, cleansing my heart and making it open to the possibility of hope. I had finally connected with my mother on a real and deeper level. In that moment I did not understand everything, but now I knew that my life meant something to someone here on earth. My mother's compassion in that moment proved to me that there was more to her than I had realized. Perhaps she had been wearing a façade all this time. Perhaps her true nature was hidden by the pain and suffering of her own life.

My father and brother did not come to me that day. The men in our family were stoic and unemotional. Tears were seen as a sign of weakness. I didn't care about all of this on that day. I cried because it cleansed me of my pain and it freed me to experience the love and compassion of my mother and sister. I felt so healed and liberated from it. At the same time, I sensed that my father was affected by what happened on that day but he was not able to express it. I never did talk to my brother about it but I knew deep down that he also suffered from all of the violence and negativity and was saddened by what had happened.

Extreme negativity can push us to the edge where we believe there is no hope. Sometimes we believe the only way out is to end it all. For those who do not get the help they require, they oftentimes do end it all. Others are not so fortunate. It is my desire through sharing my story, that more people will be assisted and shown that they are loved and appreciated.

CHAPTER 3

Society's Definition of Success

The day I chose hope instead of despair marked my search for meaning in life in earnest. I had many questions but no answers. I had been religious and somewhat spiritual until my grandmother died. I wasn't sure what to do but I knew I wasn't happy with my life and that I needed to change. I needed to find myself. I also felt the need to prove to everyone that they were wrong: I was not a stupid and worthless person. The love of my mother and sister motivated me because now I had hope. I decided to work hard and do well in school and make something of myself. I wanted to reinvent myself and show the world that rejects like me could contribute to society and deserved a chance like everyone else.

But reinvent myself into what? I had no idea what to do with my life but I did know that I wanted a career where I could help people. I went to junior college and met with a career counselor who interviewed me and advised me to take a test to see what careers would be good for me. The results revealed a number of careers: a lawyer, priest, physical therapist, occupational therapist, and teacher. Occupational Therapy appealed to me and after some research and doing some volunteer work in that area, I decided to pursue a career in Occupational Therapy. I liked it because it seemed holistic: one needed knowledge in science, kinesiology, neuro-anatomy, and activity analysis while at the same time be creative in helping the individual restore function by choosing the appropriate therapy, exercise or intrinsically motivating activity. I was really into the body/mind connection and holistic healing.

I applied for the occupational therapy program at San Jose State University, was accepted, and began studying there in 1985. I was ready to get out of San Francisco and start a new life. I moved into the dorm, met people from all walks of life, and started to make friends with all sorts of people; I kept an open mind to everybody. I had one female friend who would hang out with me from time to time. She was a quiet, soft-spoken and shy Japanese girl. She was a simple but kind person. She seemed to gravitate to me for some reason unbeknownst to me. She appeared to be a hardworking and studious person. I liked talking with her because she seemed to be very gentle and non-judgmental. She wasn't very emotional and seemed mellow. I thought we were going to be good friends one day.

Unfortunately, that day never came. It was announced in my woodworking class that she had committed suicide. My eyes began to swell and burn in sorrow and pain. Tears overcame my vision and soon all I could see was a big blur. All of the pain from my own attempt to end my life burst to the surface again. I felt an overwhelming sense of guilt. If someone had been there in her darkest hour would she have changed her mind? If we all had been better friends would that have helped? Did she have too much pressure to make it in school? Did she feel out of place and felt she didn't belong? Did she feel like a reject that no one loved? I was helpless and there were no answers.

I began to question the meaning of life again. I wondered why I hadn't noticed that she was in such a painful place. I did sense that she was lonely but she was hard to reach because she was so withdrawn. I decided then to refocus on my mission to prove that society's outcasts could make it. I just knew I couldn't give up now. Somehow I felt if I could make it, I could one day help others who may be in a plight as I was in when I felt so hopeless in life. I may not have been able to help my friend but one day I might be able to find a way to help people like us in our darkest moments to find hope. That eventually became the driving force for my ultimate success in school. I took my schooling seriously and taped lectures and read and reread chapters to make sure I understood the content. I wasn't the smartest kid around, however I worked extra hard and eventually worked my way into the honor society of Phi Kappa Phi, as well as the Golden Key National Honor society.

After I graduated, a new world awaited me. I eventually got a full-time job at a major hospital in San Francisco. Unfortunately, the staff was not very welcoming to new grads. I remember how cynical the staff was, one therapist actually said to me, "Didn't you learn anything from school!" The majority of the staff there didn't seem very happy to be working. I was in disbelief why these people were even in the healthcare industry. They were not kind but mean, rude, and uncompassionate. Though I came from a dysfunctional family, I knew that we should still be kind to people, be patient, and exude compassion.

Eventually, I found an opportunity that was supportive to a new and ambitious therapist. They gave me support and guided me, resulting in my going from staff therapist to Director of Occupational Therapy within a short time. Eventually I worked my way to become the Director of Rehabilitation, a position that I maintained for about 15 years. Then I got promoted to Area Director and managed six rehab facilities at one point in my career. I took my job seriously and gave it my all. I performed well and developed a good reputation for quality rehab services.

I don't want to make it sound like everything went smoothly after I left the hospital, because I had to work hard in the beginning. Rehabilitation can be an extremely challenging field to work in.

I remember working on some of the most challenging and difficult cases. Sometimes I got so overwhelmed. Rehabilitation can be so stressful when dealing with sick and unhappy people. They can be rude, challenging, unmotivated, and negative at times. I must confess that within my first two years of employment as a therapist I wanted to give up. I talked to my friends, colleagues and supervisor but they supported me by telling me to hang in there. I was actually going to get my doctorate in chiropractic medicine because I was fed up with all the stress and demands of my job and was inspired by my friend Hector, who is a chiropractic doctor. I even went to school and took chemistry and organic chemistry in preparation for the chiropractic college. However, I decided instead to stay in Occupational Therapy. I remember my internship supervisor, Veets, telling me about a wise Chinese man who once said, "Persevere further." And I did.

In the early 90s healthcare was going through a crisis and I survived cuts by reinventing myself. I ventured out to study clinical Hypnotherapy, Acupressure, and Reiki as a possible alternative way of making money. I started to see private clients but eventually the healthcare crisis settled down. I integrated my new alternative healing skills into the rehab work I was doing. I was enjoying being a clinician and manager, but then healthcare turned into the land of corporate takeovers. There was a growing trend for many facilities to be bought up by different companies. Job stability was uncertain and quality care was no longer important. Clinicians became simply moneymaking machines.

The care was no longer clinically driven but, rather, driven by a corporate management person. There was great pressure from management on picking up long term patients for rehab if we were slow. They would send their consultants and train us on how to be creative to screen residents for therapy. Sometimes patients didn't need therapy anymore but we were strongly advised to keep them on otherwise much money would be lost. I started to resent the management team. Many times decisions were made for financial reasons on how long we should see patients and we were forced to follow it even though the person didn't know anything about the needs of the patients.

I learned how to master this corporate game quite well and management loved me for that. More corporate take-overs happened and the environment turned more ruthless and heartless. At my last job, the new company came in and started firing people without any regard for how long the person had been working there. By the end of the day 20 people were asked to leave. I was devastated for those people who were terminated. Their lives just changed overnight. Did they really have to go? Did it have to happen so abruptly? Then our new boss came in and told us how she was going to change everything and was not going to let anything or anyone get in her way. She made all of us feel like we were all expendable and if we did not share her vision then we needed to take a hike. Clearly there was no room for compassion. I stayed in this environment until I realized that it was no longer compatible with the person I wanted to be. I knew how to play the game well but was completely disgusted by it.

I eventually mustered enough courage to move on, choosing instead to start my own company so I could run it the way I thought it should be: focusing on the client and not on profits. I believed, and still do, that if we focused on quality care and we treated our clients well, the money would follow. I strived to be the support system for my staff. I told my staff that my job is to make their job as easy and smooth as possible. I really care about each of my clinicians. To me, they are more like friends and family. My business began to blossom but then the business world's sharks preyed upon some of my therapists and tried to recruit them. Fortunately, my therapists told me about it. I confronted the agency about it. Although they apologized, I found what they did unacceptable. It seems that when push comes to shove, people's true colors come out and it can be quite ugly. It is so unfortunate how so many corrupt, unethical people exist even in the healthcare industry, while at the same time they preach integrity and professionalism.

In 1989, I met a very beautiful nurse at work. I remember doing a double take after I walked by her. Any time we had a patient together, I would try to strike up a conversation. Although I did get more confidence from work, I was still shy with women. I decided to pass her a note about meeting me for lunch at a local restaurant. She was somewhat offended by my brazen action since she was from a very conservative culture. Getting a note from me was like an insult to her. She eventually said yes and we had our first lunch. Soon we went out on our official first date at Pier 39.

The more I knew her, the more I fell in love with her. I had never felt such feelings with anyone before. I did everything I could to show her my love and affection. Then one day, it came upon me in a vision that Cassandra was going to be the mother of my children and that we were meant for each other. I knew then and there and was certain that we should be together and I wanted to spend a lifetime with her. Several months passed and I eventually had the courage to propose to her and was so delighted that she accepted. I finally won my princess. It was happily ever after right? What could go wrong? Love is all it takes, right?

The first year was the hardest. We were so alike initially but yet so different due to our cultural, family and religious background. Cassandra came from a large, wealthy and close-knit family whereas I came from a small family. My father and his parents had wealth but were extremely frugal. My father lived a very simple life and we weren't a very intimate family and my parents weren't religious at all. There was no expression of love, support, or affection in our family. We just had to be obedient and stay out of my father's path. Cassandra came from a supportive and nurturing family and I came from an abusive and dysfunctional family.

It was not a surprise when our two worlds eventually collided and created the perfect storm of doom for us. When the honeymoon phase wore off, our true colors started to shine through. All the issues of my early years started to surface. The years of abuse started to take control of me. My inadequacy and low self-esteem seemed more evident. I used to get so angry and irritated when my wife would get so many phone calls every day. It seemed like she was a celebrity and I was nothing. I must confess that I had high expectations for my wife. I see now that they were unrealistic in retrospect.

I expected my wife to know my cultural etiquette without telling her what was expected and what needed to be done in different situations. For instance, in my culture we are expected to offer tea to our guest or elders who visit. As the months passed, more issues surfaced. Soon we were arguing like my parents. Had I become my father? I had a very bad temper like my father. Little issues would seem so monumental. If my wife forgot to pour tea for my mom, I would just throw a fit and be angry the rest of the day. I was self- righteous and narrow minded. I was explosive and became a very mean person in our first year.

Overall, however, we enjoyed married life. We seemed to complement each other well despite my low self-esteem and volatile temper. I used to call myself stupid all the time when I made a mistake but Cassandra cleverly helped me get over that. She decided one day to tell me she would charge me a dollar each time I would put myself down. Within a few days, I was no longer calling myself stupid. It took the next decade or so for me to deal with my attitude and anger but Cassandra was extremely patient and tolerant. In retrospect, I can remember the sadness she felt coming from a large loving family and then living with my drama.

Despite our difficult adjustment in the first year, we always loved each other and eventually my wife became pregnant with our first child. I was so excited about the news but was somewhat apprehensive. I didn't have any special training and didn't have any good role models in my life to guide me. I was so afraid I would become my father and history would repeat itself. A part of me also felt we were too young to start a family. I felt that my family did not prepare me at all for parenthood. I pondered long and deep on my readiness to be a father. Finally, I released all fear and was just appreciative that God gave us this precious life. I told myself I would do my best to give my child a better life than I had, knowing that there remained within me a lot of childhood baggage that could affect me as a new parent that I had gotten from my own parents.

I wanted to work on myself to be better for my wife and my future child. I knew I had to somehow deal with my own conflicts with my parents before I could even deal with my own child because I would be perpetuating another generation of a child with conflicts. I decided to seek professional help and found a caring MFT (Marriage Family Therapist), Matthew Poulsen. He taught me how to challenge my thought patterns. He also helped me to understand and realize that my parents were not perfect but that they did the best they could with what they had. After a short time, I felt I was ready to take on the challenge of parenthood.

The great and glorious day finally came when my wife gave birth to our first child. Our baby girl was so adorable. Words cannot express the feelings I felt inside. She was a true miracle and blessing indeed. However, I was so afraid of carrying her because I have been known to be such a klutz. Cassandra reassured me that everything would be ok and slowly transferred our little angel to me. I held her very carefully and gingerly but was very uptight and apprehensive. As I looked into her eyes a great peace overcame me. She was such a beautiful angel God had sent us. I was just mesmerized by her. I was so happy to now have a complete family.

We kept working hard while raising our daughter and were able to amass enough money to purchase a home. We searched high and low for a house and community we felt would be a great environment to raise a family. Our search eventually led us to a nice community in Danville. The school systems were great and the city was beautiful and safe. We lived in a two story Mediterranean style home. Cassandra's mother moved in with us to help us raise our daughter. As the honeymoon phase of our new baby and new home wore off, we began living for real now. Conflicts started to emerge with Cassandra, her mom, work, and I.

Cassandra and I became workaholics to pay for our new mortgage. Cassandra is a very hard worker and quite intelligent. She got promoted to become Assistant Director of Nursing after working for three months. She did well and soon was promoted to be the Director of Nursing at a 99-bed rehab facility. Although it was a great career move, it was a high demand position. Essentially, it was a 24-hour job, with many long and late nights of over time. She would even get calls in the middle of the night and even weekends.

Needless to say, it put a strain on our relationship. I was no better. I was working on my career as a rehabilitation director at the facility where we met. The two of us became the dynamic duo at the facility. But by the time we got home, we were exhausted and were like strangers living under the same roof. However, Cassandra always had energy for our daughter and never ran out of love to give her. I had no energy by the time I came home. I was always exhausted. I would fall asleep due to fatigue and stress from work and the stress of family responsibilities. I became irritable and would get upset easily.

On top of all this, Cassandra's mother didn't make things easier. She had come to live with us when our daughter was born. The arrangement seemed like a good idea because we needed childcare since we both worked full-time and Cassandra's mother could bond with her granddaughter. Her mother was supportive in the beginning but then I noticed a change. Our daughter was almost three years old and I told my mother-in-law to let her feed herself so she could learn how to be more independent. My mother-in-law just ignored my request. This started to happen on a regular basis with other things related to my daughter. It appeared that Cassandra's mother had total disregard to my parenting requests and concerns. This infuriated me and so I brought this to the attention of my wife, who was reluctant to deal with her mother. It was like my mother-in-law had this magical spell over my wife. She would sink into profound sadness whenever she would even think about talking to her mother.

I was persistent and eventually Cassandra did confront her mother. My mother-in-law did not take it well and went ballistic. She over-dramatized the situation by calling her son to pick her up. Eventually she cooled off but then she became passive aggressive with me. We had to figure out this childcare situation. We tried to get my mother to help but it was obvious that she was out of practice so we couldn't count on her. We didn't want to hire a stranger to babysit and so we decided to make the situation with Cassandra's mother work but things got worse.

My mother-in-law became a strain on our marriage. She would ignore me when I would greet her and continued to do as she pleased with our daughter as well as our home. She called her other children in the Philippines to tell them how awful I was and how bad we were treating her. I had to bite my tongue and grit my teeth and bear with the situation. Then when she became rude to friends and family who visited our home, I was furious. It was one thing for her to do that to me but when she did it to our guests, I lost it. I told my wife that I could not stand it anymore. Things had gotten so bad that this time my wife had no choice but to deal with her mother. When Cassandra approached her mother this second time about the issues, her mother threatened to leave us. And she followed through this time.

She went back to the Philippines and stayed there for a couple of months. Then she called us complaining about how unhappy she was and begged us to allow her to return. I was reluctant to agree to it because things had gotten better between Cassandra and I after her mother left. I offered a diplomatic solution to Cassandra. I suggested her mother could stay with us a few days a week and then stay at her brother's house a few days a week. Unfortunately, we did not receive any support from any of her family members. I was extremely disappointed by this. Apparently, she has been known to be difficult to live with. I was stuck between a rock and a hard place. If I said no to Cassandra's mother, I would be the bad guy again even though I didn't do anything wrong other than try to take care of my daughter. If I said yes, Cassandra's mother again would be a thorn in our relationship. Eventually, I succumbed and Cassandra's mother came back to live with us. I did feel sorry for her mother and we needed the childcare.

In 1994 my wife got pregnant again but this time it was a boy. The joy and happiness of a second child boosted our relationship. When he was born we were fearful that our daughter might be jealous with her new brother but she wasn't. She was very happy to see him and instantly went to him to greet and welcome him to our family. It was touching to see the love our daughter had for her brother. As Cassandra lay there exhausted, I could see her contentment and happiness for giving birth to our son. We were so happy to have him join our family. By this time, I had enough experience with handling young ones that I confidently picked up our son and cradled him against my arms.

After he came into our lives, Cassandra and I began to drift apart again. Now there were five people in the family including Cassandra's mother. Cassandra was committed to her work, the children, and family but I felt there was nothing left for me. Any intimate moments seemed to frustrate her because she was simply exhausted. I held up my duties as a husband but felt neglected and alone in our relationship. When I married Cassandra, she was my best friend. After we started a family, she got so busy and I had no one to talk to. I never regretted having our kids. They were the best things that ever happened to me. Having children enriched my life and gave my life more depth and meaning. They gave me a new level joy and appreciation of life and responsibility. I just felt as though I had lost my best friend. We still loved each other but it wasn't the same.

I persevered until we hit our seven-year anniversary. Withdrawn, irritable, and passive aggressive, I was preoccupied with our failing relationship. I know I was difficult to live with because I was always on the edge. Cassandra and I argued more and more. These arguments escalated into yelling and harsh verbal assaults on each other. Cassandra was on the verge of a major meltdown, especially when I left the house because I couldn't handle it anymore. Our home environment had become volatile. Then we began fighting in front of the children. I remember how sad our daughter was when it happened. She was so young yet she tried to comfort Cassandra from drowning in despair. It was then that I realized history was repeating itself. We had become what I had dreaded most. I had become my father and Cassandra had become my mother. We had loved each other so much so how could we have reached this breaking point? I was doing to my children what my parents had done to me. How could this be happening? It seemed the only direction for us was divorce.

Our marriage was falling apart; another major low point in my life. I felt like if I didn't do something, we would lose everything my wife and I had built together. I was determined to alter this negative destiny. I put aside my pride and went to Cassandra to apologize. She seemed to half-heartedly accept my apology. I was afraid that her heart had frozen over and there would be no way for me to break through.

As we started to talk, I explored why Cassandra reacted to the fights so adversely. It turns out that she also had baggage she brought into the relationship. She was traumatized when her dad had left her family when she was a child. When I left the house whenever we argued, she would regress and in a way and re-lived the trauma of the past which prove too emotionally devastating. I promised never to do that again and made her promise to never to reach the meltdown point again. We both came to an agreement that our children and their emotional well-being was a priority.

Every day from then on we tried to work on our relationship. After a few weeks, Cassandra allowed her heart to melt. Her pride and anger slowly abated. I would reach out to hold her hand and she would reciprocate but her movements were somewhat guarded. I could feel the quiver in her fingers as we started to interlace our fingers gingerly together with great passion. The intensity of love was still there waiting to burst forth. Once our fingers met, I could feel the depth and intensity of Cassandra's love and knew, at that moment, that we were a family again.

As we climbed up the ladder of success, we would purchase things that we thought a successful person should have. We bought our second house in 2001 as the nation started to recover from 9/11. We used it as a rental property. We bought stocks in the 90s and 2000 and everything seemed to be doing well financially. Our plan was to buy and sell homes and make profits from the soaring real estate market and we would have an early retirement. People were making significant money in a short time from the real estate market. We started to put money down in so-called good buys locally as well as out of state. We even thought about purchasing real estate overseas. We were really doing well and the sky seemed to be the limit. We suddenly had all the material comforts we ever wanted. Eventually we had achieved the "American dream."

Although I owned and ran my own business, the stress would sometimes get to me. What was most difficult to deal with was the behavior of people on my staff that I trusted and relied on. When my daughter went into college, she had to move out of state. I was hoping to help her move into the dorm and help her get set up. Unfortunately, one of therapists resigned and declined to help me when I needed her to cover patient treatments so I could help my daughter. This woman and her husband were family friends. I went to their wedding. We vacationed together. I brought her into my company when she didn't have work. After she left, I found out that she went to work for the agencies we were doing business with, essentially going to work for a competitor. I understand that people have to do what is best for their career but I was in shock. Where did her integrity, professionalism, and friendship go?

During the same time period, a colleague of mine told me he was interested in working for me. I gave him a lot of business and kept him busy. He seemed professional and trustworthy. When I hired him, he told me he was involved in various groups and organizations including a fraternity group and a distinguished organization in a church group. I was impressed because the groups he associated with were reputable. I even told him I was hiring him because the groups he was part of attract people with integrity and honor. He ended up approaching one of our contracted agencies to seek employment. I knew the agency administrator quite well so she called me to tell me how unprofessional he was to seek employment with them knowing we do business with them.

When I confronted him about this, he did not deny it but tried to defend himself. He then abandoned his patients and let his work drop. I remember thinking to myself *why is this happening with my staff?* I had been supportive and appreciative of my staff. I started to lose faith in humanity. I was about ready to quit my business and just say *"screw it!"* I turned to my wife for support and she offered what help she could but was limited by her work and commitment to the family. She was supportive of the idea of me giving up my business if the stress proved too overwhelming. Fortunately, I stuck it out and kept my business but it was very stressful.

What I noticed about the American dream is that there is a price to pay for all the success. I was working late hours and so was my wife. Despite how busy we were, we always made sure we were able to participate with all the kid's activities. We went to every swim meet, school meeting, dance performance, track meet, and gave our love and support to our children in all that they did. The children united our relationship but keeping up with all their activities was extremely stressful. I can't believe how my wife and I were able to work, manage our home, and be our kids' taxi drivers all those years.

Sometimes I wished my wife and I had simple jobs, less activities, and fewer things. If I did not have to maintain our lifestyle, I wouldn't have to work so hard. I would have been much more mellow and peaceful; the dynamics at home would be much different. Perhaps my wife and I would have had more years of happiness. I wondered why life was so complicated, stressful, and intense. I wished I could run away from all of this and start my life all over again but do it differently or wished I could just press a reset button and reinvent myself. If I had to do it again, I would save more money and spend a lot less. I would put more money into our children's education. I would spend more time with family and friends and less on work. I would live a simple life. Unfortunately, I had to deal with the life that I created. Many times I felt more like a prisoner to the life I created.

Again I questioned the meaning of life. We are born, we work hard, achieve material success, take care of our kids, they grow up, and then we die. Was that it? Would anyone remember me? Would anyone care whether I came into this world or not? I would just be another statistic in life. There has to be more meaning in life? I refused to believe that this was all there was to life. Despite having all the material comforts of life, a great family, a nice house, cars, modern conveniences, I still felt empty. My soul was devoid of any meaning and substance. I believed that there was *real* happiness out there but at this point in my life it was just an elusive dream.

CHAPTER 4

Hardship Can Be a Catalyst for Healing

Although I was angry with my father most of my life, I saw things differently after I started my family. It's funny how you don't really know what things are like until you experience them yourself, like becoming a father. People tell you all the time, even your parents may say, "Just wait until you grow up and have children of your own." But you don't get it until you are in that experience. Being a father, or a parent, is a life-altering experience. I can only imagine what my father felt with all of his emotional baggage so I slowly began to appreciate him for the fact that he had been through it, just like me. I learned to accept him the way he was but saw how it was possible to have a happy loving family. Soon I realized how the family I was born into was lacking love and that maybe if my father and mother had a good dose of it things would have been different.

When my daughter was born, I wanted her grandparents to be a part of our lives so we planned events and invited our family to our home for Thanksgiving, Christmas, birthday parties, christenings, baptisms, or other events. We would have a party for any reason so we could get the family together. Our new home became the cornerstone of family gatherings. Occasionally, I would watch my parents at these events interacting with my daughter and soon after my son. My heart would melt when I'd see them frozen in time joking with my children or just being with them. It felt like all the hurt and anger from the past was washed away.

During that time my father, brother and I had a wonderful experience on one special Father's Day. We were at my brother's house and just sitting and relaxing when my brother offered me a cigar. My brother is quite the cigar aficionado. He is very proud of the collection he has of fine cigars. I wanted to try it but I also wanted to make sure my father was included so I asked my brother to see if my father wanted one, and to my surprise he did. After we lit our cigars, we puffed and wafted it to savor the taste and aroma. Up until this moment, the three of us had not spent a whole lot of time together. Growing up, my father seemed to favor my brother because he didn't have the trouble I did catching on to things and was much smarter. My brother was good with tools where I was not. I always felt like the outcast. My brother and I were never really close either.

However, when we puffed our cigars together, I felt it was an opportunity that elevated me to the same level as my brother. I felt like an equal for once in my life. I felt like we were finally connecting as brothers and father and son. It was truly a wonderful and memorable experience. As we puffed our cigars, we relaxed and talked about dinner, cigars, and life. It was the first time we had been together and had a good time. I likened this experience to when Native American Indians smoked the peace pipe. I felt a genuine connection to my brother and father, it was like we shared a Zen moment—all three of our minds were relaxed and were just enjoying being with each other. This is the first time I felt an absence of the ego in all three of us. It was truly a Divine moment that I will never forget.

Over the years that followed, my father and I started to communicate more and have more of a healthy father and son relationship. It was not easy at first, but with practice we were able to have some good conversations about anything and eventually got to the point where we enjoyed each other's company. I remember visiting my father in Chinatown and he would always offer to make me the best brew of coffee from his percolator. We sipped coffee together as we talked about family, life, and other things. It struck me that love really could heal old wounds.

After my father retired, he seemed to get sick more often. No one really thought anything of it. I think I just assumed it was a case of him getting older. In the 90s, my parents went on a cruise to the Mediterranean and when they returned my father looked so feeble and emaciated. We didn't know what had happened to him so he went to the doctor and seemed to go in and out of hospitals for a while. Eventually he was diagnosed with lung cancer and was hospitalized for prolonged periods.

We visited him frequently when he was in the hospital. We fed him, joked with him to cheer him up and offered whatever support we could give. But he became depressed and withdrawn anyway, and despite all the support and medical care, his health deteriorated rapidly. One day I went to see him and I checked in with the nurses to get an update. Apparently, his physician had come in earlier and stated that my father was doing well. I was happy with this news and as I walked in to see him, I was shocked to see his condition. His skin color was ashen, he looked emaciated, and he didn't appear to notice me when I spoke to him. It seemed like my father's life force was draining away every moment I stood there. Tears began to accumulate around eyes but I had to control them from coming out further. I wanted to run to a room alone and cry but I couldn't. I had to contain myself in front of my father, my mother, my wife, and our children. I had to control myself to give hope to my father and calm my family's anxiety with the situation.

I cannot explain it but I knew my father was on the brink of death. I called the rest of my family and told them to come and see my father. Shortly thereafter a pulmonologist saw my father and informed us that he didn't have much time. I spent time alone with my father comforting him. I knew his time was short and that I had to make every last minute count so I made the best use of my time. I was already a mess inside knowing my father was about to die. Despite the pain and hurt my father caused me during most of my early years, I still loved him. I believed there was something more to him and that deep down inside he was a great man. I tried my best to control my tears but something deep inside compelled me to say these words, "I forgive you for all the things of the past. I love you and accept you the way you are." As he took in these words, I could see tears in his eyes.

Love and forgiveness said in earnest can be so powerful. After I said it, I felt light and free. He tried to respond but it was difficult for him, I could see that he was frustrated. He struggled and struggled until he finally gave up. I even tried to make a quick communication board but he was drifting away. It was apparent that he could not communicate anymore so I gave him some acupressure massage on his third eye point. Then he closed his eyes. He seemed relaxed and serene. I left the room to convene with my family and give them an update. Shortly thereafter, I could hear him coughing and the nurses rushed in. When they were done and left the room, I decided to go in with my sister. We saw his listless body lying there in the bed. He was gone.

Tears flowed down my eyes and onto my cheeks like a stream of water flowing down violently from a severe weather storm. I had never cried so hard or long in my life. Nothing could prepare me for his death. Just knowing that his spirit was gone made me feel so empty but, the moments we shared when I forgave him was probably the tenderest moment we had ever shared with each other. I took a chance because I felt that my father was special deep down inside despite the hard facade he wore for many years. After I said what I said, I felt so liberated. It was as if the iron fist he held on me lost its grip and gave way to a more tender side of my father, but I couldn't forget his inability to say his last words to me.

My father's funeral was held at a mortuary in Chinatown about a week after he passed away. As my family and I arrived at the mortuary, the car alarm went off while the engine was still on. It only lasted for about five to 10 seconds then stopped. Not a second later my pager started beeping but I knew I turned it off before we left for the funeral. I finally had to take the battery out for it to stop. It was strange. After the funeral we went home and things got even stranger.

Our refrigerator broke the day before we went to the funeral. I was planning to fix it after my father's funeral. However, when we returned home I went to get something from the refrigerator and discovered that it was now working. If my father had been alive, he would have fixed the refrigerator so I wondered...the car alarm, the beeper, and now the refrigerator. Was my father doing all of this? The very moment I had that thought I got a little freaked out by it. I decided to go upstairs to retire but felt a cool breeze go through me as I walked up the stairs. The hairs on my arm and back of my neck rose so I ran up the stairs and into my room. As I entered my bedroom, I noticed that it smelled like cigarette smoke. I didn't smoke, neither did my wife, and the windows were closed—but my father smoked. My wife came into the room and smelled the cigarette smoke too. I finally realized that this wasn't all in my mind.

I accepted that my father was trying to communicate with me, just as he did in the hospital when he couldn't speak. I sat down on the floor next to my bed and reflected on the good memories I had of him and our wonderful moment before his death. I didn't feel scared anymore but felt a sense of peace and contentment. My father and I had finally connected at a deeper spiritual level. One year would pass before I felt my father's presence again. I would always know it was him when the room smelled like cigarette again.

I was fortunate to see my father transform from a human time bomb to the father I always knew he was deep inside. He had become a very charming father who loved to joke and socialize. He became a father that I could come to for support and have a fairly intelligent conversation. What I noticed about my father in his later years was that he really was deep and profound, while also being gentle and not too overbearing with his opinion. This is the father I will honor and remember for the rest of my life. His visits after his physical departure showed the true Divine nature of his being. These encounters with my father's presence comforted me because even though he wasn't physically here, I knew he was out there somewhere watching over us. He knows that I love him despite what happened when I was younger. His presence reactivated my quest for meaning in life. Now I felt ready to begin rebuilding my life and start becoming the person I was meant to be.

PART II

What Can Be

*"In this universe it is love that binds everything together.
Love is the very foundation, beauty, and fulfillment in life."*
—Amma (Mata Amritanandamayi Devi)

CHAPTER 5

Rebirth and Discovery

Many of us brought up in the West use medicine for every ailment. I did too. I used pills or medicine to treat asthma, depression, anxiety, pain, bacterial infection, and the common cold. Medicine has a purpose—if I didn't have medicine to treat my asthma I might have died. I remember having severe asthma attacks where I was gasping for air. I would start to panic but when I finally got my medication and inhaled, my breathing became more normal again.

When it comes to depression, anxiety, or emotional pain, medication might not always be the best answer but it does help. It is not just a matter of popping a pill and feeling better instantly. For me, it was a process of trial and error. When the dosage and strength of my medication was low, I felt no benefit. When it was too high, I was spaced out or drowsy. I worked closely with my doctor and eventually found the right dosage. However, even with the right dosage, sometimes the dosage had to be changed because my body would get used to it and not get the same benefits it once had. As a result, the doctor would have to adjust the medication again which sometimes would bring on more side effects. Side effects can sometimes be mild and sometimes severe. Sometimes I would take one medication for a while and it would no longer work then I would have to switch to a new one.

I thought to myself, *will I have to continue taking medication for the rest of my life?* That idea didn't appeal to me. The medication helped treat my symptoms but they did nothing to resolve the root cause of my issues. When life would get more challenging, my emotions would be affected. I noticed a correlation between the amount of stress in my life and how bad I felt. The more life issues, the more worse I felt and I would have to take stronger medication. It was a vicious cycle. I knew that I had to break that cycle and find an alternate way. I needed to find deeper and more permanent solutions. I needed to get to the cause and root of my unhappiness. So I went to talk therapy to better understand what was going on in my life and how I could deal with life's issues and challenges more effectively.

I worked with a wonderful and amazing therapist. Silvia Morgan M.A. and MFT, was instrumental in helping me find strategies to deal with stress and life issues. She helped me elucidate my thought patterns and challenge my perceptions. She gave me useful tools to change how I dealt with stress. She helped me find my own solutions and how to face many of my fears. And of deep importance, she would tell me that no matter how bad things seemed there are always options. Her support, guidance, insights and teachings were quite helpful and within a short time, I started to get back on track in life.

Because psychology was one of my favorite subjects in college, I was intrigued with how the mind works and the relationship between body, mind and spirit. I realized how much of my unhappiness or anger were automatic reactions to situations in life. I knew that the trauma I went through in my early years still lingered somewhere in the corner of my subconscious mind. I was aware that this trauma affected my behavior and thinking at a level where I was not even aware. I knew I had to now work on healing my subconscious mind in order for me to truly be free. Fortunately, I met two people who specialized in this area.

Lisa Halpin is a Consulting Hypnotist, DCH (Doctorate in Clinical Hypnotherapy), BCH (Board Certified Hypnotist). She is a Neuro Linguistic Programming (NLP) practitioner, the originator of HypnoCoach®, and a National Guild of Hypnotists (NGH) advisory board member. Through hypnosis, I was able to heal the hurt child I once was and reprogram my subconscious mind to accept more positive suggestions and ideas to move me forward. She gave me strong positive hypnotic suggestions that made a huge impact on me. She even made me a set of self-hypnosis tapes that I use from time to time to reinforce the positive changes I made. Through her custom tapes, I was able to reach many of my goals in life.

The second person who helped my sub-consciousness is Susan Lee, RN, and International NeiGong Director. She is an advanced emotional freedom technique (EFT) trainer, was a Senior Editor for China Central Television, International News, and the host of her own talk show, English Outlook Magazine. She has won several international awards for documentaries on AIDS and other topics. Susan Lee used NeiGong techniques to help me release lingering emotional pains of the past. Besides helping me to heal the pain, she also taught me how to activate Qi energy. She also taught me how to protect and shield myself as a healer by creating myself an energy field when working with clients. But then she went above and beyond in helping me to heal further. She sensed that there was not a complete spiritual and emotional closure with my father. I had almost forgotten my father since his death. She offered to go with me to the cemetery to pay the proper respect to my father following Chinese traditions. She wanted to give me emotional support in that spiritual healing moment. The ceremony was simple but yet profound. We brought things typically used to pay respect: wine, his picture, food, and incense. I felt a real connection to my father as I honored him, paid respect as I prayed in front of his tombstone for love, and peace and forgiveness for not remembering to still honor his memory.

Because of the work I did with these two wonderful healers, I was not so much under the influence of my subconscious mind. I experienced less interference from inner conflicts that had once functioned within my subconscious mind. Now I had more control of my mind but every now and then I was haunted by thoughts of my father on his deathbed and his inability to tell me his last words, his visits after he died, my friend's suicide, and my own thoughts of suicide. I still felt that there had to be more to life than just being free from pain and suffering. I felt there was something deeper and more spiritual that was missing from my life. Perhaps the answer was in religion again?

When I was young, religion gave me a great deal of peace but I stopped going to church after my grandmother passed away. I went to church with my wife to support her. Going to Sunday mass became the thing to do to get spiritually recharged. Anytime I had a problem, I would pray about it in church but that was the extent of my spiritual life. I always felt God was so far away and too busy. I imagined that he was probably overwhelmed with trillions of thoughts and prayer requests every minute. Perhaps that was why my grandmother and father died because my prayer request didn't make it into his voice mail or inbox because it was already full. Then a kind and caring friend of mine, Angelica Heller, encouraged me to reconnect with God again through prayer. I started to pray to God at that point and looking to him for guidance again as I had done prior to my grandmother's death. Angelica was also concerned about my spiritual growth so she suggested I learn about Joel Osteen, an American preacher, televangelist, author, and the Pastor of Lakewood Church in Houston, Texas. His ministry reaches over seven million broadcast media viewers weekly in over 100 nations around the world. Interesting enough, my mother who speaks limited English told me around the same time that she enjoyed watching his program. She was captivated by his oratory abilities.

Now that really got my attention so I watched his broadcast sermon on television. He spoke from his heart and it was so motivating. I wanted to learn more about him so I bought his CD, *Living in Favor, Abundance, and Joy*. I listened to them all the time and integrated them into my life. His principles taught me how to live a better life to be closer to God. Later, I met a spiritual guide later who also told me to watch Joel Osteen. Perhaps God was using all these people to tell me to hear the message I needed to hear from Joel that would help me on my spiritual journey?

I owned my own company; work took up the majority of my time and the rest I spent with my family so my social life was non-existent. I decided to explore Facebook as a way to connect with people. I was able to connect with people from all walks of life and have met some genuine and supportive people. Although the friendship may have started somewhat superficial in the beginning, these friends have turned out to be more supportive to me than some of my "real friends." During some really challenging times in my life, these special friends have stuck by me to give me the love and support that made a huge difference in helping me make it through. One of these friends I met on Facebook, Averi Torres, had a fascinating and diverse background. She is a corporate, government, celebrity and personal psychic medium as well as a global spiritual teacher, doing readings for over 50 years. She is known as one of the top 10 best psychics in the world and has helped thousands of people worldwide including Fortune 500 executives, Hollywood celebrities, congressmen, and U.S. Presidents.

She is also a very humble Divine being. I was drawn to her and knew deep down inside she would be the one to be able to help me with my various concerns in life. Soon I started to consult with her regarding business, personal, and spiritual matters. She was quite sound with her all advice but I had one burning question. I needed to find out what my father was trying to tell me before he died. She said without hesitation that he was trying to tell me to take care of my mother. You have no idea how healing this was to my heart. Deep down inside he really did care for my mother. That only taught me to love my father even more and realized that he was really a man of greatness and love. Averi encouraged me to move forward on my spiritual journey and was perhaps the first and only person who cared about my spiritual well-being at that time. I have consulted her on various important times in my life and she never ceases to amaze me with her accuracy and sound advice.

We continue to be friends to this very day and her advice, guidance and consultations have always been quite valuable, insightful and helpful. After Averi sparked my spiritual interest, I went and did everything I could to learn how to be more spiritual and follow the path that leads towards God. That process was over a period of two years. During that time, I prayed, meditated, read all sorts of spiritual books, attended spiritual seminars, and learned from any willing spiritual guides I could find. I got to a point where I was able to have Oneness with God, the Universe and Cosmos. Through daily meditation, living a spiritual life and my openness to the universe, I eventually was able to discover my own spiritual Gurus or guides from within.

As I became more spiritual, my life began to transform. I saw a direct connection between what I did and how it affected my spiritual life. I started to become more compassionate with people. I started to have more gratitude. I accepted myself and others just as they were. I became more willing to serve and was less attached to the material world. I also felt content with whatever life dealt out to me, and started to put all my faith in God and trust him with all my heart and mind. My emotional outbursts drifted away. Many people, especially my family, noticed the difference in my demeanor and how I seemed to have this new found peace and happiness.

Two people have had a huge influence on me: Joel Osteen, which I had explored earlier, and Dr. Wayne Dyer, an internationally renowned author and speaker in the field of self-development. I have to drive a lot for my job so I bought audio CDs. I listened to CD after CD over and over learning from these spiritual icons. I started to digest, process, and integrate much of my learning into my daily practice until it became a part of me. I meditated daily, and then one day had a gentle prompting from within to read books that would further my depth in spiritual evolution like *Tao Te Ching*, *Hua Hu Ching*, *Bhagavad Gita*, and books from Deepak Chopra. The more I read and integrated what I learned into my life, the more peace and happiness I would find. I felt like the universe was supporting me as I was awakening to the process. My life had more meaning and I saw more value in what I did. But I have discovered that to be a true master, the learning and discovery must never stop. I keep exploring and keep learning.

In early 2013, I was speaking with a friend of mine, Indika Thakur, about the yogi guru Paramahansa Yogananda and the guru Sathya Sai Baba from India. I told her how I had visited Yogananda's hermitage in the Lake Shrine Temple and Retreat in Pacific Palisades. It was an amazing and spiritual experience to spend the afternoon there. I had gone there after reading the amazing book, *Autobiography of a Yogi*. Yogananda loved God dearly and lived an exemplary life. He has been so instrumental in igniting my spiritual path. I still attend functions sponsored by the organization he started in 1920, the Self-Realization Fellowship. Indika mentioned that she had not read his book nor had she ever been to the Lake Shrine but told me she met Sathya Sai Baba when she was in her late teens. Apparently, being in his presence was like meeting the Divine. I had learned about him shortly after he died in 2011 from an Indian client of mine. Then she asked if I had heard about Mata Amritanandamayi, also known as Amma, which means "mother" in Hindu. I searched the Internet and discovered that she was still alive.

I believed that if I could meet a living saint I could see firsthand what is so special about them, if anything at all. To me, meeting a saint was like getting as close as you can to meeting God. If everything I had read were true, meeting Amma would validate for me that it was possible for a human being to access the Divine. I was skeptical so I told myself not to expect much so I would not be disappointed. I read more about her and learned that she was a humanitarian, philanthropist, and was known as the "hugging saint." She calls her hugs "darshan," which is a Sanskrit term meaning "to see." I guess most spiritual masters are seen but not touched. Amma's hugging started when she was a teenager as she used it to help comfort people who were either lonely or suffering in her village. She has continued to hug even to this day and it is estimated that she has embraced over 32 million people.

I was so eager to meet her in person and was delighted to see that she had a tour schedule, and that she was going to be in my area. My wife and I made plans to go see Amma. We were the first people to show up. While we were waiting we began talking with one of her followers. He was getting the stage ready and had just finished. We told him that it was our first time meeting Amma. He spoke about how she affected his life in a positive way with such conviction it was like seeing a Divine light in his eyes.

When Amma arrived, the energy in the temple shifted. Her aura flooded the hall with a calmness and Divine love that exuded from her presence. We had the perfect seats, only three to five feet away from Amma. Then I felt an overwhelming sense of peace fall over me, like a warm blanket. She was unpretentious, humble, genuine, and full of grace. She did not utter a word but we could all feel her Divine energy and love.

Shortly after, we were led to a beautiful meditation by one of leaders of the group and when it concluded, my wife and I were escorted to her holiness. We were guided to her and lowered onto our knees to receive our Darshan. I was the second person to receive Darshan that day. As she embraced me and hugged me, she chanted. A huge wave of compassion and unconditional love hit my soul. It was as if I was a dying plant seeking water and suddenly I was bathed in a shower of unconditional, pure love. It was like my spark of light within was suddenly given a surge of pure Divine oxygen that ignited my soul to the purity and oneness with God. It was so overwhelming that all I could do was weep uncontrollably.

My wife also received a Darshan after me. I didn't expect my wife to have any reaction because she was even more of a skeptic than I was. To my surprise, she cried like I never heard her cry before. I knew she was overwhelmed by the unconditional love that she felt also. After we were done, some of her followers had to help us get up and walk us over to an alternate area where we kneeled down in close proximity of Amma. I felt in that moment she knew me and understood the thirst of my soul. I was allowed to stay near her as others proceeded to meet her for a great duration. As I knelt, I could hear a song playing in the background and recall the lyrics: *This is my dream….This is my Prayer….Love is the Answer….Love is the way.*

Love is what I had been searching for all my life. I wanted it from my parents, wife, siblings, close friends, teachers, coworkers, children, and others. I just wanted to be loved and accepted. I worked hard to be successful so that maybe one day, I would get noticed and maybe I could earn love and acceptance. Unfortunately, I never felt that anyone loved me unconditionally, except my grandmother. The tears continued to flow as I absorbed unconditional love from the Darshan Amma gave me. A lifetime of thirst was finally quenched in that moment for me. My soul finally drank from the Divine goblet of love that heals and empowers. It was one of most important days of my life. From that day forward, I knew that love was the answer I had been seeking for all my life and that the love of God was more powerful than I had realized.

The next day, I returned to take part in a special event called the Devi Bhava with Amma. It is a special event that celebrates the feminine aspect of God, and God's unconditional love and compassion for all humanity. I discovered that we were eligible to get our own mantra from Amma. A mantra is a Sanskrit term for a sound, syllable, word, or group of words that is considered capable of creating a spiritual transformation. Its use and type varies according to the school and philosophy associated with the mantra. According to Swami Veda Bharati, mantras are "sonar forms of the forces of divinity" and have been used for centuries as an aid to focus the mind during meditation as well as to produce changes in the consciousness. Apparently, it is not easy to get a mantra. Some disciples have had to wait months to years before their guru would consider giving it to them. Disciples had to endure hardship to prove their worthiness before receiving a mantra. I felt so privileged and honored to be given the opportunity to receive a mantra from her holiness.

There were thousands of people who attended this event. To receive my mantra, I had to stand in a special line. There was another line where people were waiting to get their Darshan. They were the priority so I had to wait until I was guided to Amma to receive my own personal and spiritually infused mantra. While waiting, I enjoyed the festive and spiritual environment. Musicians played ancient Indian instruments and sang Indian songs as the spiritual event went all day and night. Finally, the moment came when I was escorted to Amma to get my mantra. Amma gave me another Darshan, and I felt the same peace and contentment I had before. I was given my mantra and instructed to proceed upstairs to get training since it was in Sanskrit. They taught me how to pronounce it, how to use it, and how to chant it with the Mala, which is a string of beads used in Buddhism and Hinduism for reciting prayers. As I practiced, the words seem to resonate with me and it felt so natural saying it. I chanted that evening and have continued to do so every day to draw closer to God and keep me connected to Amma at a metaphysical level.

After my experience with Amma, I was clear about my calling in life: helping others find joy, peace, and happiness by discovering the Divinity within and without. I dedicated my life to spiritual growth so that I could be a servant and messenger bringing a message of love and hope to everyone I meet on life's journey. As I was waking up from my spiritual hibernation, I was inspired to write down 18 principles of happiness and success that I practiced daily. Information began to flood my mind as I was writing, like someone had poured spiritual nitro into my crown chakra. Divine information was coming in at warp speed. Sometimes I had to record it so that I would not forget it because I could not write as fast as the universe wanted to download into my mind. I realized that this was bigger than me. I was an instrument and the Divine had taken over, that is when I dared to imagine this book.

CHAPTER 6

The 18 Principles for Happiness, Peace, and True Success

Through years of searching, being open to the process, and practice, I have come to 18 principles that have helped me in my transformation. I practice these principles daily so I am continually making that shift to inner happiness, peace, and true success in every moment. I offer them here for you to discover and use toward your own journey.

1. Acceptance

The journey begins with acceptance. You must learn to accept yourself for who you are, and not what you pretend to be or what you want to be. You are love in physical form as created by the Divine. You are perfect in every way, right now and for all time. We step into acceptance once we manifest the Divinity from within us and learn to accept the unconditional love of God just because we came into this world. You will realize that you are not judged because you don't measure up to a certain ideal, but rather that you are loved just because you exist. There is only one you. You are here to find your purpose and fulfill it. You find your purpose through alignment with the Divine.

When I was searching and studying Dr. Wayne Dyer's work, one nugget of wisdom struck me in the audio CD, Making the Shift, and it was this: "I am in this world but I am not of this world." At many times during my life, I felt like a mutant like in the X-Men comics. They were different from humans because of genetic mutations that make them express certain powers. Although I cannot command the weather, beam lights out of my eyes, walk through walls, read minds, or shoot indestructible steel blades from my knuckles, I felt like the mutants because I didn't feel accepted by people and like I didn't belong anywhere. I felt different. I was different in the way I looked. People would think I was not Chinese.

I have been called various ethnicities including Hawaiian, Japanese, Korean, Canadian Indian, Filipino, Burmese, Chilean, and even one Irish man thought I had some Irish blood because I assimilated his accent in a few minutes. The most bizarre ethnicity I've been called is African-Chinese. Recently an Indian client asked if I was from Southern India, specifically from Kerala. I couldn't really relate to most of my friends at a deep level. I always felt odd. I never really felt accepted by anyone and that people rarely understood me. I talked, thought, perceived the world differently than most of the people I met. To many people I seemed odd or eccentric. It was a lonely world to be in.

During the majority of my marriage, I operated from my ego and fear. This created so much pain and strife in our lives. I tried to change my wife into someone I thought she should be but the more I tried to change her, the more conflicts we had. When I accepted her for who she is, love stepped in and that saved our marriage. She is now beginning her own spiritual journey and is meditating with me. It is so beautiful to see her learn to accept herself as well.

I had difficulty accepting my mother-in-law. She had been so negative and such a source of strife in our marriage. During my spiritual evolution and awakening, I decided to accept her the way she is. I realize that she has her own problems and inner demons that no one can resolve except herself. Despite her flaws, I learned to focus on all the good that she does and learned to ignore everything else. I practiced loving her and accepting her unconditionally. I was consistent in loving her and accepting despite her negative behaviors. Then one day, she began to change. She started to show more interest in my life and we now we have a mutual respect for one another. My greatest gratitude for her is that because of her I get to spend my life with my wonderful wife and friend. My mother-in-law has told my wife that she enjoys living with us and that she really respects me now.

By accepting my children as God made them, they no longer felt threatened by me and are beginning to gravitate towards me. Now I have a great relationship with my daughter and my son is starting to open up to me.

When you accept yourself, you free up the space in yourself to accept others as they are without trying to change them. I was finally able to accept my parents for who they were. I was no longer a prisoner to the fear and anger I had towards them. I was free to step into my own power. This acceptance not only freed me but also helped my mother recover from her illness and reclaim her life. I also believe that through acceptance my father was able to feel peace at the end even though for most of his life he felt anger and resentment.

One of the biggest challenges is accepting yourself as you are no matter how others perceive you. Many of us are concerned about what other people think. It does not matter. The only thing that matters is what you think about yourself because it will protect you from ignorance. Many people I have met in my life believe their race is the best, or the most pure. I used to think I was a mutt who didn't belong anywhere. Now I am proud of my diversity and heritage. I am proud to be Chinese and an American. Because of my diverse heritage, I feel I can perceive the world from dual perspectives. What I once thought was a weakness now becomes my strength because I am open to other cultures. There is goodness in all cultures. Yes, I am an Asian-American but I am part of a bigger group too, the human race. By embracing our common ground—our humanity—we can accept our differences and learn from one another.

When I meet people, I see the beauty in a person. I see what we have in common and look forward to learning the differences. When I meet someone, I try to learn about their culture and maybe learn a word, a phrase or two in their language; this usually helps me connect better with the person. I use this same principle throughout my life and it has helped me with my career as well as my work and personal relationships. I have clients from all ethnicities. When I meet them, I try to greet them in their language. The clients really appreciate it and I can build good rapport quickly by showing an interest in their culture and language. I have watched a man transform from angry to gentle once he realized I knew something of his religion, language, and culture.

Many of my Indian friends and clients have been quite open about discussing about spiritual matters. It was through a client that I was exposed to Sathya Sai Baba and the book, *Autobiography of a Yogi*. One client was even so kind to give me a picture of Sathya Sai Baba to hang on my wall when I told her how I respected this great Saint. Others have discussed about their Sikh faith and opened my eyes to the bravery of their great Gurus. I was also exposed to the book, *The Bhagavad Gita*, from an Indian stranger who came to my house years ago in Chinatown and gave the holy book to me. The first time I opened the book, I felt dizzy as I looked at the pictures of Krishna. I didn't even know who he was at the time. I put the book away for almost decades. A spiritual person from India decades later told me it was a holy book and that I had that response because I was not quite ready yet to read it. When I began to become more spiritual, I began to read it and found great messages of truth in it. It is truly a profound and Divine book which serves as a great guide to find Divinity.

By accepting yourself and others you become more open to the possibilities in life. Acceptance allows us to experience much more and helps us to realize we are one human race, and are much more similar than different. However, we can take it a step further; we are all actually Divine spiritual beings. We may all have different shapes, sizes, colors and genders but we are all truly Divine spiritual beings in different levels of awareness. Acceptance can liberate you from the prison of negativity and self-hate. When you can truly accept yourself, you will see the beauty in everything and everyone. You will experience a depth of peace and happiness you once thought impossible. I believe this is the next critical stage in our evolution as humans.

2. Spirituality

Spirituality to me is a way of life that leads us to our source. It is the path that will end all suffering and help us to realize true, Divine unconditional love. It is the path that liberates us from the delusions of the material world. It is the path that liberates the soul so it can return to its true nature. There is no conversion in spirituality, as in having to convert to a certain doctrine or dogma, the only transformation that happens with spirituality is you become more of who you truly are once all the layers of humanity that have been peeled away and bring forth the Divine being that we truly are.

Religion is actually a good place to start on a journey to discover spirituality. Religion is good if it teaches principles that uplift, inspire, and enlighten. It should help individuals grow and thrive with the goal of nourishing the Divinity within. Belonging to a religious group that resonates with you and supports your spiritual growth, can be helpful as you begin your spiritual journey. It is important to be aware of the negative side of any particular religions. It should teach and support love and acceptance rather than judge and condemn. A church predicated on God's love, forgiveness, grace, and compassion and service to one another is a good place to start. We must all learn to have tolerance to one another's religion.

All spiritual masters, like Buddha, Jesus, Sathya Sai Baba, and Amma, teach acceptance as a basic stepping-stone to reach the Divine level of spirituality. Buddha taught tolerance. He would tell his disciples that if the other religions or teachings were reasonable and rational, they should respect those principles. He even told his disciples not to accept his teachings easily but to consider them carefully to determine for themselves whether it was practical or not. Because of this philosophy, practicing Buddhists tend to accept anyone into their religion with open arms. What is important in Buddhism is not so much the dogma but living the teachings as a way of life. I agree with the Buddhists in their view of tolerance and being opened with what religion people have. I am always interested to hear why people believe what they do. I believe as they do that spirituality is a way of life.

Paul Ferrini, an ordained minister, author of 40 life-changing books, and speaker says in his book, *Love Without Conditions*, "divisions into religions are relics of this world." Ferrini wrote that, "A true follower of Jesus does not advocate any kind of separation." Instead he describes Jesus as being compassionate, tolerant, forgiving, and loving to all beings regardless of their religions or their walk in life.

I truly believe that all of us are just part of one big family. We may look, dress, speak, and eat differently but we all breathe the same air, live on the same planet, and are born the same way. We are all part of the human race and have the spark of God's light within us. At our most pure level, we are energetic light beings that come from the same source. In order for us to return to our true Divine nature, we need to live a life of love, forgiveness and tolerance. It is in unity that brings us closer to our source. In being divisive, we are living a life ruled by the ego which only leads to a life of chaos, greed and discord which is not the life that God or Jesus would want us to have.

In the Bible, Jesus said:

> But I say to you who hear, love your enemies, do good to those who hate you, bless those who curse you, pray for those who abuse you. To one who strikes you on the cheek, offer the other also, and from one who takes away your cloak do not withhold your tunic either. Give to everyone who begs from you, and from one who takes away your goods do not demand them back. And as you wish that others would do to you, do so to them. (Luke 6:27-36, English Standard Version)

Sathya Sai Baba taught acceptance for all religions. His work was about helping individuals to discover their Divinity within. His words encouraged his followers to be tolerant:

There is only one religion, the religion of love;

There is only one language, the language of the
Heart;
There is only one caste, the caste of Humanity;
There is only one law, the law of Karma;
There is only one God, He is Omnipresent.1

And these words:

*Let the different faiths exist, let them flourish,
let the glory of God be sung in all languages in a
variety of tunes. That should be the ideal. Respect
the differences between the faiths and recognize
them as valid so far as they do not extinguish the
flames of unity.*[1]

Amma also accepts everyone and people of all faith,
but says that her religion is love. Her website says that she
has never asked anyone to change their religion but only to
contemplate the essential principles of their own faith and
to try to live accordingly.

God is omnipresent. He is all around, within and
without all things and all people. I believe that God has
different manifestations depending on the needs of the
people and hence there are different religions and faith. We
all believe in the one God and are all part of the same
Divine family. The one truth is spread throughout all the
religions. Many religions feel they have the one truth. We
can say either all religions are wrong or all religion is right.
However, I feel it is at the intersection of all religions and
mysticisms that one truth exists. It is man's interpretation
of all the holy books that affect the clarity of the message
of God. The ultimate truth must ultimately be sought from
within in the stillness of the mind, unadulterated by the ego
and worldly attachments and desires. However, one must
establish a basic foundation either by a spiritual group,
guru, spiritual guide or church. Church has helped me in

my journey and provided so many people with happiness and peace.

I have been in Buddhist temples, Hindu temples, Lutheran churches, Catholic churches, Pentecostal churches, Episcopal churches, etc. and have felt the presence of God in all of them. Perhaps we can all learn to accept one another and draw close to God in our own way but realize that there is more we can do for our salvation, freedom, and happiness.

I attend church and it gives me a sense of community. Many times as I sing, I get choked up because the Divine touches my heart through the music and lyrics. It's interesting to me that I never had this problem in past when I would sing in church until I became spiritual. I believe this is because I was "religious" and not spiritual. People may go to church every Sunday but during the rest of the week they live a very different life full of anger, judgment, and fear. Being spiritual is not only for Sundays or holidays. It is a way of life. We do not earn gold stars in some big book God has for our perfect attendance and involvement with church related activities. We do earn peace and happiness by living a life of love in the Divine. We can be spiritual by how we treat one another with love, compassion, forgiveness, and integrity. We must learn to be of service to one another in all that we do.

For those who want to take a different path to spirituality, finding a spiritual guide, spiritual group, or a guru, can help make the journey easier. We all need help with our spiritual development. In fact, to move to a higher spiritual level, we do need help. In the spiritual realm, there is an active positive and negative force within and without.

For most of us, we walk through this world unconscious to our Divinity. We do not even know we are lost but we do feel the pain, emptiness, and fear. This is why a guide can be instrumental in helping us find our way and as you have just read it can be very important in keeping us on the path of light towards God.

Churches are in a good position to help people get even closer to God. If more churches and spiritual leaders could help its parishioners and members learn to meditate and get deeper into spiritual teachings, imagine the impact it would have on the world in bringing people even closer to God. When we reach the day when we (churches, mystics and all spiritual beings) are all going towards the one source and path to the light of God and realize and accept that we are all from the same Divine family and cooperate with one another, unity and love will prevail and help the world to bring forth peace, love and happiness to all sentient beings.

3. Integrity

Righteousness, honesty, character, virtue, and morality are all components of integrity. They are all ingredients for living a life that is worth more than simply just taking up space and oxygen. We must be just, fair, and righteous but not self-righteous. We need to embrace integrity not for a reward or recognition but just for the sake of doing good. On his CD, *Good, Better, Blessed: Living with Purpose, Power, and Passion*, Joel Osteen gives an example of integrity when he talks about what happens when a bank teller gives you too much money. Are you going to say something and return the money or are you going to say, *"Thank you Jesus, you did it again!"* People laugh, but many of us think God is just sitting there waiting for opportunities to give us extra bonuses for being good. It doesn't work that way.

Sometimes I have to ride the F-line from the Ferry Building to Fisherman's Wharf in San Francisco. The terminal is so crowded that a lot of people enter from the rear, and I am no exception. When you enter this way, it's easy to simply board the street car without paying the fare.

A lot of people do it. It's tempting for me to not pay too but I know the city gets its money from the public transit service. If I didn't pay, I would save four dollars and I and can buy myself a Caramel Macchiato at Starbucks and maybe even a snack. But I pay because it is the right thing to do. My gain would have been Muni's loss. If more and more people skipped paying fares, it would cost the city millions. If we all pitch in, the city could have more money for the police department, public works, and other special programs. All of us doing good and being honest can make a difference in our families, neighborhood, community, society, civilization, and ourselves.

We can also have integrity when we drive. For many people, our cars become extensions of ourselves. Our cars become an extension of our personal space as well. As such, we many times are protective of our space when we drive. I was no exception until I started my spiritual awakening. During my younger days, I was driving like I was a Formula One race car driver. Unfortunately, you can't apply those same principles on the public road. I also did all the no-no's of driving. I was not courteous on the road. When people were trying to change lanes, I would not let them. If they cut in front of me, I would tailgate them and high beam them or honk at them. I was driving with my ego on nitro. I would get mad at anyone who would be too slow or get into my personal space. I guess you might describe me as being somewhat aggressive. I was always honking my horn for one crazy thing or another. Amazingly enough, my children are the complete opposite and follow proper driving etiquette.

My pattern of driving only made me an aggressive and angry person. In retrospect, I must have irritated so many people and spread so much negativity all around. Fortunately, as I changed and evolved spiritually, I realized the impact on the world on everything I do including driving. There is a chain reaction to everything we do in life. As I drive daily I still see many people who are very disrespectful and reckless on the road. I see people who tailgate, cut people off, refuse to allow people to merge in traffic. I see violence and aggression with one driver to another due to misunderstanding, bad attitude, ego or pride. Driving is a privilege and a social responsibility. When we drive, we should be cognizant all of us are part of a Divine creation. We all have different functions and roles to do in our little world but our world is interrelated and interconnected to others. When we drive, we should have respect for all on the road.

We should discipline ourselves while we drive to spread love, forgiveness and compassion when we drive. When we see someone in need, help in any way possible. If it is unsafe to help, call for help and pray for the individual. If someone cuts in front of us, avoid anger and retaliation. Instead give the person more space and pray for the individual's safety. Perhaps the person is driving fast due to an emergency.

Do not tailgate anyone for it creates a negative energy and is also very dangerous. One step on the brakes of the driver in front can cause an accident and change your reality forever as well as many others who are just innocent casualties. When that accident happens, it not only affects the lives of those directly involved, but it also creates traffic congestion affecting others from reaching their destination, potentially affecting yet more, who may be depending on them. Soon local businesses are affected and the effect can be widespread depending on the severity of the accident or congestion.

If we treat all those we meet on the road or elsewhere with integrity by choosing to spread love, compassion, forgiveness, and positivity then the road of life that connects all of us will begin flow smoothly and allow all of us to follow thru on our special roles, duties and functions in life.

Do good with what we say, write, and do to others wherever we may be—on the road, home, school, work, etc. At the end of the day we all have to look at ourselves in the mirror and face the truth: what we do to others is how we treat God.

There are many other ways we can show integrity as well. Nowadays there is so much bullying that goes on in schools. Unfortunately, many times it leads to a negative consequence of someone losing their life. If we have knowledge of such an activity going on, we need to support the person, try to get the person some help or report it to someone of authority. Ignoring it doesn't make it go away. If that person was your daughter, son or friend, I am sure you would act differently. We must remember that person is also a face of God and as such we should treat that and all life with respect. All life is precious.

In a family, it is common for parents to treat each sibling differently. Many times that creates disharmony and rivalry. As parents, we must do our best to love all our children the same and do our best to impart our love to each child. When children feel they are loved, they are less likely to be jealous and spiteful with their sibling and others. It is easy to gravitate towards one child more than another because some may have more positive traits than others. However, each child is different and has come into existence for a particular Divine agenda. They need that love as a basic ingredient to help slowly nurture that spark of light to come forward. We must not compete with one another for it only destroys an opportunity for a beautiful relationship with our siblings. We must love our parents and treat them with respect because despite how bad they may seem, they too need love and are also a face of God.

We must have integrity even at work. It is so easy to just slack off on a job when no one is watching. It is easy for us to just surf the web for our own follies when we are at work, text our friends or even sleep on the job. Rather than do that, it is better if we can make ourselves available to do another project or help another colleague. Ask how you can be of service. This type of action only leads to greater job stability and better work ethics. Who knows, you may even end up getting a promotion.

We must have integrity in all that we do including our homeowner responsibilities. I have witnessed people who had good jobs walk away from their home because the real estate market was crashing. Instead of selling it, they claim they couldn't afford it, and yet they turn around and buy a more expensive house. It just doesn't make sense and in the end, the person has just cheated the system and put a financial burden on the bank that now owns the house. The consequence extends to the government, the people and the economy. Many people live their lives cheating the system any way they can. They never see the implications of their actions and are more concerned about themselves and how to get ahead at all costs. We must be more cognizant of the implications of our actions beyond ourselves. In the end, all of us must face that consequence of all our actions.

4. Love

Through my spiritual studies, I have found that the greatest gift of Divinity is love. Divine love is unconditional. This is the kind of love I am speaking about, not what most of us think in terms of romantic love, or love for your family, a sport, a hobby, a country, etc. Divine, unconditional love is difficult to describe in terms of human language. It is vast, unending, and eternal. It has the power to heal physical, emotional and spiritual dysfunctions. It transcends human understanding and has the power to create miracles. It is the love that saves us and liberates us. It is something not to be defined but to be experienced in our oneness with God. There is nothing we need to do or change to be loved. We don't need to be beautiful, rich or famous to be loved.

All creation is loved unconditionally for just being here. Many people who have had a near death experience (NDE) state that when they go to the other side, they feel and experience complete and unconditional love. Dr. Raymond A. Moody expounds about all this and more in his book, *Life after Life: The Investigation of a Phenomenon—Survival of Bodily Death.* Give and receive love unconditionally for it is the food for the soul. The source of all Divine love is God. Find God and you will find love and true happiness.

I did not love myself for most of life due to all the memes I had learned from my parents, teachers, and society. A meme (pronounced "meem") is basically an idea, behavior, or style that spreads from person to person within a culture and in some cases, that meme becomes the accepted definition of the idea, behavior, or style for that culture. I believed that I was not worthy of love. I worked hard on eliminating as much memes in my life. I did hypnosis to release the emotional hold of them. I learned a lot from Dr. Wayne Dyer on how to be cognizant of memes and cognitive processing and how to shift my mind and be free of being a prisoner to these memes. Sometimes they seem so real that we believe they reside in us.

Love for our self is vital to our health and well-being. I believe God intends Divine love to be the foundation for all creation, because without it, growth is unable to happen. There is physical proof for this everywhere but one that strikes me is in the book, *The Hidden Messages in Water,* by Dr. Masaru Emoto. Dr. Emoto was able to show the effect of the word "love" written on a cup of frozen water. He wrote the word on the inside of the cup, facing the water. The frozen water sat for three hours then he took pictures of the beautiful crystals that formed. It did not matter what languages the word was written in, the frozen water formed beautiful crystals with the word, "love," or other positive words. When negative words were put on the cup like "you fool!" or "You make me sick," the crystals were malformed and fragmented. Since the human body is made up as much as 90 percent water, imagine the effects on our bodies when we do not love ourselves, or when we think negative thoughts about ourselves. It makes one wonder if some diseases are caused simply because there is a lack of self-love. Controversial? Maybe. Truth? Maybe. Dr. Emoto did more interesting and eye-opening research in his book including how positive intentions or prayers have the same effects on frozen water noting that they formed beautiful crystals.

Love extends not only to all sentient beings but also to all of God's creation, great and small. Somehow I came across a video on YouTube about the story of a lion named Christian. Later, I discovered the story behind the video. In 1969, John Rendall and Ace Burke purchased a lion cub from Harrods department store in London, England, which had acquired the cub from a zoo that went out of business. The two men raised the lion cub and named him Christian. They gave lots of love to him and he became quite tame and lovable. He became a part of the family. Eventually, Christian outgrew his human surroundings so John and Ace returned the lion to the wild in Africa.

One year after Christian was released into the wild, John and Ace decided to go looking for him to see whether Christian would remember them. They ended up finding Christian, who had two lionesses with him. They approached him cautiously since Christian appeared intimidating at first. But as they got closer, Christian recognized them and leapt at them, hugged them and wagged his tail like a happy dog seeing the return of his old friend. The lionesses eventually also accepted John and Ace as well. Divine love unites all creation. In the absence of fear and in the fullness of love, all things are possible in the realm of Divinity.

One of my wishes for my family was for them to experience the unconditional love of a pet. They were not interested at all, even my kids. I didn't give up though. I brought up the idea again and again since I had a pet once as a kid. I have seen and experienced how the unconditional love of a pet can be quite healing. One day we were fortunate that an opportunity came up and we acquired a rescue puppy. He was a Chihuahua, Pekingese, and Yorkie mix. We all fell in love with the little fellow, Max.

Life with Max was great, until one day he became aggressive. It started after a grooming appointment. While the groomer was trying to trim his toenails, he started growling and biting the groomer. I can only guess that the groomer cut too deep and hurt him causing him to start distrusting the world. He became increasingly aggressive. We had hired a dog trainer but that didn't seem to help Max. We consulted our veterinarian, Dr. Kim, about our options. Max growled and barked at him. I wondered if there was any hope for Max but Dr. Kim was willing to work with us and Max on a behavioral management program.

As we brought in Max, he growled and barked at him, but he was undaunted by Max display of agitation and anger and methodically took him out of the cage. We discussed whether he should be put under but I could tell he was emotionally troubled by my question. He stated Max was too young and I could see the compassion he showed to him. He left the treatment room and came back after a while and stated that he was willing to work with his staff in behavioral management with Max. He was very sincere and really wanted to help and hence we proceeded to let them work with him to help him become a member of our family. Much work was done with helping Max and the staff at the veterinarian's office was extremely supportive. We also hired a dog whisperer to work with him.

We encouraged Max with love and positive behavior reinforcement. My daughter was very patient with him no matter how aggressive he became. She encouraged positive behavior and loved him anyway. Each month Max's behavior would improve. Then one day Max became aggressive with me. I decided to offer my hand to him out of love trusting that he would demonstrate positive behavior rather than aggressive behavior. I can't explain it but something within told me it was safe. In the past, me holding out my hand would have meant a negative outcome for me. So, I held out my hand and Max growled and he started to charge towards me. I had faith and trust in Max. Then it seemed as if all his anger and fear dissipated as he reached my hand. I petted him and he licked my hand. From then on we had a mutual understanding. He relinquished his Alpha role and allowed me be the leader of the pack.

He continued to show progress and has become my best friend and a great family pet. It is very interesting that it is usually the unconditional love of our pets that is beneficial to people. In our case, it is through the unconditional love of the staff at our local vet, Dr. Kim, Erin, Christina, Jessica and staff, the dog whisperer and our family that has given Max the chance to live and manifest the love that he has to share as well. We are so pleased and delighted that Max has finally found his place in our family through all the love he received. Again, in the absence of fear and in the midst of love all things are possible.

Just as much as we need to connect with Divine, unconditional love, we need touch. Touch is a basic human need and an expression of love. In fact, studies have shown that when a baby is not held or touched, that baby does not develop as well as children who are held, touched, and cuddled. For me, growing in an Asian culture hugging or cuddling was not something we practiced. Some cultures are comfortable expressing love with kisses or hugs.

Fortunately, I picked up a habit of hugging from my some of my Latin and Filipino friends and in-laws.

As I have grown spiritually, I have expressed my love with my family through touch even though it was not practiced in our home when I was young. When I am walking with my family, I often put my arms around them to express how much I care for them. Words can say much but our touch can show depth to our words and soul. When my father was dying, I stroked his forehead and did acupressure to help him relax. It was my way of nonverbally expressing my love and gratitude to him. I know he appreciated it and it was a way for us to bond when words escaped us.

For the past three years, I have been taking care of my mother when she fell ill. She was severely depressed, had body aches and was fainting quite frequently. She had lost a lot of weight and at one point weighed less than 90 pounds. She had generalized weakness, trouble walking and even had trouble carrying a conversation. She was withdrawn and apathetic to the world. She was barely hanging on to life, but refused to get help or live with us or in an assisted living facility.

I took care of my mother by visiting her every week taking care of her medications, shopping for her, and giving her unconditional love and healing energies. I would massage her shoulders and after her initial reluctance, she would relax and absorb the benefits. One day she asked me why I was so kind to her. I just smiled and said, "Because I love you." Many months later, she blurted out in Chinese, "I thank God for giving me you." Keep in mind my mother is not religious at all so I was surprised by what she said. I asked her why she said it. She told me because I help her, give her my time, and do what others won't do. I continued to visit her and give her my love and slowly she started to heal both physically and spiritually. Then she started telling me that she wanted to help needy people and give donations to the poor. She even told me that she had walked by a homeless man, stopped, and gave him some money. I could not believe my ears. My mother has never wanted to help the needy and now here she is doing it. She now regularly visits her elderly friend in need and asks me if I can drive her to drop off food to her as well as to her other friends. I am amazed at the caring person she was becoming.

Recently, my mother and I were shopping at a local flower shop. The owner was very kind and generous. My mother was so touched, she hugged and kissed him on the cheek and told him he was kind. I was shocked but delighted. A few days later, I was helping my mother. I had to drive her somewhere and my wife went with us. While I was gone a few moments, they spoke in my absence. We dropped off my mother later that day and my wife said, "Blake, do you know that I talked with your mom today? I told her that you loved her very much." Then my wife said my mother's response was, "I know. I love him too." I was deeply touched by her words. I always knew that she loved me but to hear those words was quite healing for me. It only validated how love truly heals, unites, and makes the impossible possible.

I believe it was Divine, unconditional love in the form of words, touch, action, and prayers that led to my mom full recovery but I never expected her spiritual healing as well. Perhaps my mother needed unconditional love as much as I needed it to help her awaken the Divinity within. When I am walking with my family, many times I would put my arms around my daughter or wife to express my love and care for them. It has helped our relationship. Sometimes when my wife is asleep, I gently stroke her face to express my love and affection. I am sure her soul deeply appreciates it.

Much of the healing I have facilitated through my work and my company has been done through touch. I set aside my ego and allow Divinity to work through my hands for my client. I have witnessed miraculous healing in both humans and animals. I believe that this does not come from me, I am simply the instrument and the Divine delivers the unconditional love that heals. One elderly woman I worked with had dementia and was bedridden. She was unable to interact with her world because her muscles had atrophied to where she had poor head and neck control. Her neck muscles were tight and her chin had essentially been on her chest for past six months. She also had no movement in her left arm and hand. All previous therapies and medication had shown no results in improving her condition. I worked on her neck muscles, did acupressure on her left arm and hand, and prayed while sending her love and light. Almost immediately she started to move her left hand then she became aware of her neck muscles and looked up at her relatives standing in the room. The family was amazed by her transformation.

The healing power of love goes beyond human beings. It goes to all of God's creation including his canine friends. My other dog is Tamiko. She once developed a bad limp throughout the day. I quickly picked her up and worked on her right hip using the same methods as I had mentioned earlier but did it over a longer period of time. After I was done I returned her to the floor and she had improved by 75%. The next day, I gave her one more session and then her limp was gone. I am just a facilitator. Healing is an expression of Divine Love. I am only an instrument of God for healing.

Many times my clients who have had a stroke have no movement in their limbs. Since I have been an occupational therapist for 26 years, I can usually tell what the potential of return is but I never put restrictions on what the patient can achieve that is up to God. I allow my hand to work where it needs to go and I become one with my client for a while before I proceed with the various neurological facilitation techniques as well as Eastern techniques coupled with positive intentions of love. My clients and family are just flabbergasted by the results I get as some of my clients begin to move his or her shoulder, elbow, wrist, hand, or finger. Sometimes the result is so dramatic while other times it is so subtle and minute that only a trained eye or hand can feel it. Those are the times I can even detect a small group of muscle fibers contracting.

Whether the progress is great, small, or nil is irrelevant. I am happy either way to be an instrument for God to use to help improve the individual's quality of life or facilitate recovery. I am just a facilitator and not a healer. The healing comes from the Divinity within and without the individual. Things work better when my ego is not involved. I do not concerned with the outcome but allow Divinity to work through me. The human body is designed to heal itself and will do so in the right conditions. I just help create a scenario where the conditions are optimal for an individual to heal him or herself.

Mother Theresa once said, "Not all of us can do great things. But we can do small things with great love." By giving of ourselves and sharing our love, we discover the Divinity that is within all of us. Spreading love is our work while on Earth. It truly heals our body, mind and spirit.

5. Laughter

A friend once gave me a sticker that read, "Some of us have one of those days but you have one of those lives." I thought this was funny but in a way, it was true. Laughter has always helped me get through many difficult years in life. By finding the humor in even the most challenging situations, we put a positive spin on a potentially negative situation.

Laughter therapy is increasing in its use and popularity because it really helps. National Public Radio did a special segment on it by interviewing Steve Wilson,

President of the World Laughter Tour. Wilson stated that laughter therapy helps relieve stress and improves things like blood flow and digestion. It's getting so popular that even the Pentagon is training military families to use it. According to Wilson, laughter helps relieve muscular tension, lowers the heart rate, and, helps treat depression.[2]

Laughter is also contagious in a good way. One weekend my wife and I had lunch with a good friend from college and her husband. We hadn't seen them for a while and it was so great to catch up with them. It didn't take long before we were sharing stories and laughing. We laughed so hard that we cried. The same thing happens when I get together with my buddy, Paul. After we're done trying to unlock the mysteries of the universe, we joke a lot. Paul knows a lot about metaphysics and has inspired me to learn more about the subject. Our conversations usually end up in a laugh attack that can last as long as 10-15 minutes. Our laugh attacks recharge me. I feel so refreshed, energized, and alive. A good laugh can do that for you.

Laughter releases worries, fears, and pain. In my yoga class at Umang's Wellness Haven, we always end the class with a great belly laugh exercise, which always brightens my day. When we laugh, the child within us comes out and plays. According to Mencius, "The great man is he who does not lose his child's heart; the original good heart with which every man is born." I used to be so serious but once I released the child within without, I began to see the world in a whole new perspective and began to really enjoy life. So many people are so serious and find it hard to laugh. When we laugh with someone, we put our guards down and accept the other person. In the midst of laughter, our egos take a nap and we are open to the possibility of love.

6. Awareness of SIN

Most of us are aware of the definition of "sin" as taught to us in church. Through my spiritual journey, I have developed my own definition that is an acronym for S.I.N.

S—*Separation from God or Divinity*

We separate from God when the self is the center of the world. The individual is living an ego-driven life. We are given the free gift of choice. We create our own reality and our mind universe. We can choose to live our lives under the material world driven by ego gratification and never experience Divinity. We can seek financial freedom, wealth, and fame in the material world or we can seek alignment with Divinity and find true peace and happiness. Dr. Wayne Dyer has said, "You will never find meaning through your ego." When we lose our ego, we rediscover the spiritual being we are and have always been.

Most of my life, I lived an Ego driven life. I felt like I was the center of the world. I was always right and everyone else was wrong. I became a very angry and unhappy person. I was always doing things in the best interest of myself. I strove to rise to the top to become successful, buying things to fill the shallow ego I had. The more I had, the better I felt about myself. The material success only led me to lose myself. As I became disillusioned with the material success and ego and started to serve people, I began to rediscover my true self and began to really live. I find joy in serving people in all that I do. The more I serve, the more I feel closer to Divinity.

Besides serving others I meet along life's journey as well as my family, I read the Bible, pray and meditate daily and go to church which assists me in staying close to God. The more I did those things, think less of myself and allow myself to be more be of an instrument of God for healing, helping and serving, the more my life began to have true meaning and value.

I—Id

Id is a Freudian term used to describe the basic instinctual human drives. It is the source of bodily needs, wants, desires, and impulses, particularly sexual or aggressive drives. We operate on a level that only satisfies our immediate urge for something. We do what we want without discretion and concern for consequence. When we succumb to the Id, we only think about our needs and desires. We pay no regard to anything else and objectify people rather than see the Divinity in all of us.

Business targets us at this level. They find ways to sell us things to feed the Id in us; things that will bring us false joy and tap into our desires or libido. Unfortunately, many people fall prey to the slick marketing strategies of big business. I was no exception. I bought into the American dream. I would purchase whatever it was that made me look like a successful person. I developed this "got to have it" mentality. At the moment whenever I bought something fueled by this desire to have it, I would feel great. Then I would find myself feeling empty until the cycle repeated itself. This American dream, the one where you must buy something to measure up, is an elusive one. There is always something new and better to buy, and that emptiness inside never gets filled with any new thing you can buy.

Our libido is important to help procreate our species but over indulgence in it causes one to lose sight of the important things in life. It is such a powerful force in us, which needs to be tamed and managed to help and allow one to reach higher consciousness and spiritual evolution. When Mahatma Gandhi became more spiritual, he became celibate as well as many other Indian saints. I am not saying that you must be celibate so you can become more spiritually enlightened but if you allow your libido to rule over your choices and actions in life then you find it hard to have purity of mind, body and spirit as you meditate and pray. Any strong attachment to the world, whether to the flesh or material things weakens our Divine experiences and spiritual evolution. When I allow over indulgence in my libido, I begin to lose sight of what is right and wrong. It interferes in my oneness with Divinity and experiencing the "subtle truths" that Dr. Wayne Dyer talks about. As I put less value on it and manage it more, my spiritual experiences only deepens and my guides begin to manifest again. The Taoists believe that by controlling our libido we can extend our life.

Ultimately, if the Id is allowed to go astray it leads us to the path of chaos and a life devoid of Divinity and the ego becomes the center of the universe. Such a scenario and hedonistic way of life is best illustrated in F. Scott Fitzgerald's book, *The Great Gatsby*. However, if the individual gains awareness and acceptance of the spirituality and Divinity within and takes measures to change, the individual helps to reawaken the Divinity within and with some guidance and hard work can help and reclaim his or her life and become the Divine being that he or she is meant to be.

N—Negativity

Negativity is one of the greatest foes of Humankind. Memes and false beliefs by our parents, society, media, movies, or entertainment can all support, and even encourage, negativity. When we allow our mind universe to be full of dark clouds, storms, we limit our evolution and strangle the seed of Divinity. Negativity is like a virus and it is highly contagious, affecting millions and billions of people. It affects our relationships with ourselves, friends, family, partners, and communities. It affects our internal world and universe as well. Negativity causes our body to become more acidic leading to illness, disease, and even death if negativity is extreme. If we think and feel negative towards someone, it creates symptoms of stress and leads us to anxiety, depression, and anger that all weaken the immune system. If we do or act in a negative way, we spread that negativity virus. If we yell at someone, they may feel hurt and project their anger thus perpetuating negativity. We contribute to their illness in health and estrangement of their Divinity.

Until I set out consciously on my spiritual journey, I was very negative about others and myself. It limited me from finding happiness and compromised my health. I would let myself get stressed out and became anxious, irritable, and volatile. I let the little things in life bother me so much that it would ruin my day as well as my family's day. I wasn't happy the way I was and always needed reassurance from my wife. As I acted and thought negatively, I would draw in negative people in my life and would be presented with one challenge after another. Changing my mind and attitude to be more positive allowed me to have greater peace and happiness with families, friends and myself. It also improved my health and business by being more positive. Negativity is a lot like weeds, it will do everything to survive and grow back. However by staying vigilant of mind and heart through meditation, prayer, inspirational music, yoga, and eating healthily, one can recharge the positive energy easily. When we keep our mind universe positive, God is able to use us to do wonderful and amazing things to those around.

7. Visualization

All conscious manifestations begin with imagination and visualization. If you consciously and intentionally visualize and imagine, then you consciously materialize your reality. Imagination and visualization are Divine gifts we must cherish and use to make a difference in the universe within and without. Imagination is something we are born with and most of us were good at using when we were children. For many, as a part of aging, imagination takes a back seat to more practical matters and this is unfortunate because it is through imagination that some of the greatest inventions and innovations known to mankind have happened. I am sure that Orville and Wilbur Wright imagined what it would be like to fly before they even put a pen to a paper in designing the first airplane. They probably visualized it over and over again until the vision of the first design came to them. That's how it works.

Most people don't realize the power they have over their mind universe. We can choose to live in heaven or hell just by thinking, imagining, and visualizing it. We create the seasons, weather, climate and tone or color of our mind universe through our choice and imagination. Albert Einstein said that, "Imagination is more important than knowledge." He also said, "The true sign of intelligence is not knowledge but imagination." Einstein knew the power our imagination has on not only creating our physical world but also on our inner universe.

Visualization is easy to learn. It is like imagination but filled with sensory details like smells, sounds, sights, feelings, and even touch. The more detailed the visualization is, the more effective the results will be. Dr. Wayne Dyer recommends that we visualize what we want before we sleep and when we first wake up. He also says it is best to assume the feelings of the wish fulfilled. I take this to mean that the more you can really get into the feelings of your desire, the more real it becomes and the more likely you are to take actions to make it a reality.

When my kids were young, they had to do various projects for school. One of my daughter's projects in junior high was to build a miniature model of the Golden Gate Bridge. Anyone who knows me knows that building things is not one of my strengths so when she approached me for help with this project I was overwhelmed to say the least.

However, my daughter was counting on me. I had to rise to the occasion. I released all my fear and beliefs what I can or cannot do. I just imagined the completion of the project. My daughter and I built her project out of balsa wood and it ended up turning out really good. I have no idea how we did it but it all started from my imagination and visualization.

Visualization has helped my business. I would imagine it growing every day. I rarely did any marketing. Companies and employees heard about my business and sought me out. Visualization helped me to write this book. I would envision the completed book and visualize myself completing it. I kept my mind open to the universe and soon ideas and concepts started to flow with little effort.

Visualization also helped me land a role in a local theater production of *The Nutcracker*. I have been acting on stage for about three years in various roles so this was something I really wanted to do. I would imagine and visualize how nice it would be to play the role of Dr. Drosselmeyer. Under normal circumstances, I would never be considered for this part because I was not a professional at that time but I would imagine it anyway. An opportunity presented itself and I made it clear to the people involved in the production that I wanted the role. I planted the seed and didn't think much of it afterwards. I still dreamed about the role and visualized how I would perform it. Through a twist of fate, Miss Susan Blanchard, artistic director of a local ballet company, asked if I would consider the role. I was so flabbergasted that I could hardly contain myself. Inside, I was jumping up and down with joy. Coincidence? Some might think so, but I know it was largely the power of visualization which allows the Universe to align with us, our dreams and aspirations.

This role was a very special one. I did a lot of research on how to manifest the essence of the character. I memorized all of the dance steps of the ballerinas that I would interact with and choreographed my movements with them. Daily I would live, drink, and eat *The Nutcracker*. I could see it in my sleep and dreams. Finally, the day came for my debut as Dr. Drosselmeyer. I did my best through the support, guidance, and help of our fearless and wonderful leader, Miss Susan Blanchard. Professional dancers, family, friends as well as the director came up to me to congratulate me. I couldn't believe it but strangers and even high school kids wanted to pose with me after the show to take a picture. Many people stopped by and said I did a great job. It was an amazing experience I will never forget.

I think the most priceless thing to me was sharing the experience with my daughter. She has been with the dancing company prior to my joining. I got a chance to see her practice every day up close. I admired her for all her hard work and dedication. She is truly a gifted dancer. We also shared the same goal to give our all to make the show a success. The next year I reprised my role as Dr. Drosselmeyer. This time my daughter was cast as Clara, his niece. We were the father and daughter team, both with principle roles. It was the most memorable and precious moment in my life I will never forget. None of this would have happened if I did not dare to imagine. Never limit what you can do or achieve for if you can visualize and dare to imagine with conviction, the sky is the limit on the many possibilities that awaits you.

Dr. Wayne Dyer read a beautiful excerpt from Neville Goddard's book, *The Power of Awareness*, regarding imagination from the *Making the Shift* audio CD:

The great secret is a controlled imagination and a well sustained attention firmly and repeatedly focused on the object to be accomplished. It cannot be emphasized too much that by creating an ideal within your mental sphere by assuming that you are already that ideal. You identify yourself with it and thereby transform yourself into its image; thinking from the ideal instead of thinking of the ideal.

Every state is already there as mere possibilities as long as we think of them but as overpoweringly real when we think from them. This was called by the ancient teachers, *subjection to the will of God or resting in the Lord.* And the only true test of resting in the Lord is that all who do rest are inevitably transformed into the image of that in which they rest. You become according to your resigned will and your resigned will is your concept of yourself and all that you consent to and accept as true.

You assume the feeling of your wish fulfilled and continue therein takes upon yourself the results of that state not assuming the feeling of your wish fulfilled, you are ever free of the results. The truth that sets you free is that you can experience in imagination what you desire to experience in reality and by maintaining this experience in imagination; your desire will and must become an actuality.

We often waste a lot of mind energy and we don't even know it. We fill our mind universe with trash and wonder why we are not realizing our dreams. We need to focus our energy on imagining and visualizing what we want. If we are reading every magazine sent to us with things to buy, watch every shopping channel, our mind soon begins to zero in on that, rather than our dreams and heart's desires. Soon all one thinks of is buy, buy and buy. Therefore, it is important to spend our time more productively: reading books that will help us visualize and imagine our highest possible calling. Great benefit can also be attained through listening to uplifting music, entertainment, or audio CDs that nurture our mind universe.

Affirmations are another form of visualization. An affirmation is a typically a statement that is positive, personal and specific. Louise Hay, best-selling author and motivational speaker, wrote about how affirmations can literally heal you in her book, *You Can Heal Your Life*. In Joel Osteen's CD, *Good, Better, Blessed: Living with Purpose, Power and Passion*, he once talked about how his mom had terminal cancer. She posted pictures of herself when she was healthy as a visual cue to help her focus on being positive. Through her faith, motivation, prayers, and visualization, her cancer went into remission. I have taught my wife affirmations to help her with back pains which gave her relief. Positive affirmations when practiced consistently can truly heal.

8. Forgiveness

While writing this book, I was involved in a major car accident. A large truck made an abrupt illegal U-turn in front of me. He was on the right lane and I was on the left lane behind him. The truck driver all of a sudden decided to make a sharp U-turn, without warning, and turned into my lane and towards me, ramming my SUV on the right side and dragging my car across the median. He apparently didn't think anyone was on the road let alone nearby. The right side of the SUV had severe damage and was actually wedged under part of the truck. Fortunately, I didn't have a passenger on the right lest he or she be injured. The accident caused a traffic jam on both sides of the street as many onlookers slowed down to see if we needed help or were just curious. The accident blocked off one lane from each side of traffic. All this happened so fast but when the collision happened, all of a sudden everything seemed to be going in slow motion. I was shocked at what was happening but somehow knew I was going to be alright. Yet there was a moment when I thought a severe injury or even my death might result.

I believe God was with me because that day I decided to take my SUV instead of my low profile sports sedan. If I had taken the other car that day, the entire car might have been crushed under the truck and I would not be here today. After the accident, I slowly got out of my car to see if I had sustained any injuries and if the truck driver was okay. He jumped out of his truck screaming and yelling hysterically. When I realized I was fine, I thanked God for sending his guardian angels to watch over me. Life is so fragile but yet so precious. I didn't care about the car and wasn't even mad at the truck driver for causing the accident. He seemed agitated and anxious about what I was going to do. I looked at him told him that I was just happy to be alive. I smiled at him and said it could have been worse. His expression changed to one of confusion but then his demeanor changed. He was calmer. I had already forgiven him before he got out of his truck. He ended up giving me his insurance information with no resistance or hassle at all. I am sure he was expecting me to be angry but instead I greeted him with peace, forgiveness, and gratitude.

It is never too late to forgive, even when whatever has been done seems too horrific to overcome. When we hold a grudge, it keeps us imprisoned in an emotional gridlock. This may cause us to be stuck forever on the event, wrong doing, or grievance. The only way to be truly free and liberated from the bondage of emotional slavery is through forgiveness. Although we may bury our anger deep in our heart and mind and forget about it consciously, the subconscious mind doesn't forget it. It prevents us from evolving as a person and finding true happiness and peace.

Every experience in life is a learning experience. When we get mad at someone it is usually an opportunity for us to learn and grow from it if we open our mind to the lesson to be learned. Sometimes things happen over and over again until we learn. Sometimes people who cause us the most unhappiness are teachers in disguise.

I have many reasons why I could be angry at the world. I could be angry for the emotional abuse from my parents, the discrimination I faced as a child, abandonment by my church congregation, betrayal of employees, and so on. It takes a great deal of energy to harbor all this anger, and I did for a long time. But I have learned to forgive everyone, and most importantly, myself. When I forgive people, I opened my mind to give them the benefit of the doubt and try to understand them from their perspective. After I forgive them, I follow with praying for love, abundance and happiness to that person or whatever the person needs. This has helped me channel my energy in a more spiritual and productive way and help spread love and free myself. Many times people say and do things they don't mean. They do it because of their own issues. I do know this: we cannot grow, mature, evolve, and become spiritual until we learn to forgive. Forgiveness heals us physically as well as spiritually. Remember to always forgive, embrace the wisdom offered, and live with no regrets. To forgive is to be truly Divine.

9. Releasing Expectations

Expectations can be a double-edged sword. When we expect the best from others and ourselves, we often get it. The trouble comes when we expect situations or people to be a certain way, and then the reality doesn't match those expectations. We put all of our energy, hopes, and beliefs into those expectations and are disappointed or disillusioned when things don't work out the way we imagined. This causes pain and resentment because what was expected did not materialize. When we live in this ego-driven life, we alienate ourselves from God. We think we have control over our fate. We think by doing certain actions we should be guaranteed a certain outcome. Unfortunately, it doesn't always happen that way. Life likes to throw us curve balls when we least expect it and it seems to always happen for many of us. You can count on it.

Most of us, including myself, have forgotten that we are Divine and spiritual beings. We forget that the moment we are born. It takes effort and hard work to go through the self-realization process. During that spiritual evolution, we begin to realize that we are not alone and that there is Divine intelligence out there. There are countless times in my life where I should have been in a bad accident but was somehow protected.

One time I was driving home from L.A. with a friend and I just decided to take an alternate route at the last minute. I don't know why but something inside prompted me to do that. I later found out if I had stayed on the route we had started on we would have encountered a rockslide and might have been in an accident. Another example was when my wife and I were on our honeymoon, I was shopping in a store. While browsing around I decided to pause for a second at the right time then the attic stairway just fell straight down right in front of me. If I kept going it would have crushed me. I have no doubt there is Divine intelligence. We have to realize that if there is Divine intelligence out there then conceivably there is a master plan for each one of us.

Most of us, including myself, function on autopilot most of our lives. When we navigate our lives with our ego, it is like driving with a pair of dark sunglasses on at night. We can sort of see where we are going but chances are we are going to get lost or get in an accident. However, if we put our faith and trust in God, he will guide us to where we are intended to be. We just need to learn to trust in the process and strive to be one with God. We need to learn how to abdicate the duality of life and have oneness with God through prayer, devotion, meditation and living a spiritual and Divine life. I used to worry about everything in life but no longer do that. I now trust in God for I know he cares. I know as long as I walk in path of righteousness and in the light, I will always be where I am supposed to be and do what I am supposed to do.

Now I realize that sometimes things happen for a reason and we just need to look at the wonderful plan that God will be unveiling to us next. Sometimes it is easy to see and other times it takes decades to see the beautiful plan in store for us. I used to always ask God why are all these bad things happening to me? Why am I surrounded by all these negative people? Why do I have to suffer? I thought that if I did well or was a good person, I would be blessed and would always expect good things to happen but when they didn't, I was disappointed. Now I realize that bad things happen for a reason. I know there was a Divine plan that helped me become the person I am today. Through all my suffering, I have learned how to be a better person. I can now help others ease the pain and find their own path to the light that brings happiness and true success.

As a society, we have come up with rules and expectations for certain behaviors. We are taught that it is imperative to say thank you when someone gives us something. If someone does not show appreciation it is considered rude. When I analyze why I feel a need to be thanked, I realize that I want recognition to validate that I am a nice guy or special person. It has nothing to do with what was given or why it was given. It has to do with feeding the ego, and this always leads to a false sense of gratification. Through my journey I have come to realize that a deeper sense of gratification can be filled when I give rather than receive. When we give without expectation, we discover the essence of Divinity, which is a pure unconditional love. I have learned to love, give, and share for no other benefit other than being closer to Divinity. Give without expectation of praise, recognition or fame for it is truly Divine.

Most of my life I expected people to behave a certain way. I expected people to be nice to me, supportive of my book, supportive of my spiritual journey, supportive of my acting, and supportive of my accomplishments. Many times I was met with jealousy, negativity, and apathy by even some of my closest friends. I would get excited about something and friends would not show any excitement. Instead, they would just change the topic or seem to be more concerned about what they wanted to talk about.

As I evolved spiritually, I learn to forgive people and realize that they all have their own issues in life and their inability to share joy, love, and excitement has nothing to do with me. I learned to be more humble with some of my friends who may be threatened by my metamorphosis. Perhaps my friends' apathy is a lesson for me to learn about humility. Every situation is an opportunity to learn.

Many times when I do good things, I expect the universe to reward me in some way; perhaps more abundance, more spiritual gifts or visions. However, things don't always turn out that way. I have to remind myself that bad things happen not as a punishment but as part of the process of learning. Each time I learn and gain insight, I become stronger and radiate more of the light within and grow closer to God. I remind myself to do things from my heart, while not expecting to receive anything in return. I prefer to do it out of pure unconditional love. As I do that, I begin to live a more fulfilling and meaningful life.

10. Change Belief System

When I was in high school, I had so many negative beliefs that affected my outlook on life and what I was able to do. I believed that:

- I was not worthy.
- I was stupid.

- I was not attractive.
- I would never amount to anything.
- I was not smart.
- I was fat.
- I was dumb.
- I did not belong.
- I did not know how to talk.
- I did not know how to listen.

It was extremely difficult to go through high school with so much negative beliefs. Through the support of friends, my wife, and my own hard work I was able to change some of these false beliefs. It required soul searching and talking to understand the dynamics of how they were formed. I went to MFTs (Marriage Family Therapist) to help me elucidate many of my false beliefs about myself. They helped me to challenge my perceptions about my situation and my beliefs. It was eye opening and liberating. It helps to have a professional person give you feedback on the validity of our perceptions and beliefs system.

Then I went to hypnosis to release those false beliefs at the subconscious level and start reprogramming my mind with positive thoughts and beliefs. The effects of hypnosis were quite good and help me to get through many difficult times. My hypnotherapist made me my own customized hypnosis tape to help me break through the many false beliefs I still had of myself which affected how I felt about myself. Many years had passed and eventually I would occasionally regress due to adverse work environment, changes in life circumstance and issues at home. I started to do self-hypnosis again to reprogram my subconscious mind with great benefits.

I also discovered PSYCH-K. This tool developed by Robert M. Williams in 1988 is designed to help you change beliefs in your subconscious mind. In PSYCH-K, kinesiology is used to communicate with the subconscious mind. Specific body postures and movements cause neuron firings in both hemispheres of the brain, creating a state in which change can more readily occur. I found it to be an effective tool for making positive changes in behavior and thought patterns. I studied it and used as a method for helping people and had good results and look forward to studying it deeper in the future.

Life is ever changing and new experiences often give birth to new feelings, thoughts and behavior, sometimes good and sometimes bad. If life got tougher or more intense, I would have more stress and if things started to go out of my control, I started to get depressed again, believing that I was no good. When things in life smoothed out more, I would have less stress and feel better again. In the past, I had managed these conditions through medication, supplements, and exercise. The problem was, however, that the symptoms were contingent on what would happen during my day at work or with friends or family. I believed that stress and depression are just part of human life and that I just had to figure out how to live with them.

Then I had an epiphany. While listening to Dr. Wayne Dyer's *Making the Shift* CD, which I mentioned a lot in this book, I finally came to the realization that we can change our negative belief system after becoming aware of it. During one part of the audio, Dr. Dyer invited some of his audience to share their memes. One man shared about his stress and depression. Dr. Dyer says that stress is a meme. Although we feel it is so real, it is our conscious perception or judgment on any particular activity, situation and event, which decides if we are to be stressed, or not. I have always been a person who gets stressed out easily. However, once it became clear to me the power of my mind and of how it creates my mind universe through my choice I make, I began to start asserting my Divine ability to choose to release the feelings of stress and choose to smile and be happy.

I chose to think of something else more positive to change the storm in the mind. It is true that the environment and what goes on sends a stimulus to our body and mind but how we choose to perceive it is entirely up to us. It takes some practice at first but once you get the hang of it you stop reacting with thoughts like, *I am so stressed out, I am so depressed, I am so angry, I am dumb, I am not smart, or etc.* Sometimes we say it so much that it becomes a part of us. If we don't allow these thoughts to be released, they affect our mental, physical and emotional well-being. If it persists, the issues will be stored in our body and weaken our immune system or might later develop into diseases and illness. The first step is to be aware of these processes in our mind and our beliefs.

It is important to practice choosing how we want our mind universe. We do that by redirecting our thoughts. For example, if I feel anxious, depressed, or obsessed with thoughts like, *I am stupid*, I can choose to think something else like maybe a time I did something great and felt good about it. As I would immerse myself into the emotional context of the memory, I would feel more positive. What I created was a positive mental or emotional wave. I would ride that wave like a surfer as far as I can. When the negative waves start to come in again, I would think of another positive thought or memory and catch that wave for as long as I can too. We are truly the masters of our own mind universe if we choose to exert our authority and command to the vast universe within our mind. Sometimes, I command myself to be happy or to be positive. Sometimes when I am tired, I command myself to be full of energy and a little while later I feel a surge of energy.

The final step is to change our behavior to support the mind in its change. After I give myself a command to be happy or positive, I usually will follow up with some type of action or behavioral change to reinforce it. I may make a big smile as if I were happy for as long as I can. Laughing hysterically helps too whether I am truly laughing at something or not but surprisingly enough, many times after I do these things, there is a shift in how I feel and think.

What helped me ultimately change my belief system is when I started to explore a higher consciousness and awareness. Through meditation, I became one with Divinity, the universe and the cosmic. It is not an easy task but when I started to release my ego, negative thinking and emotions I began to have oneness with God. In moments of stillness, I have felt the unconditional love of God and learned to accept myself as a perfect creation of God as all of us are. Also in the midst of stillness, I receive visions and guidance to help me to stay on the path of enlightenment. Through spirituality I now walk in the path of the light and radiate the light from within. Where there is light and love, darkness dissipates and gives rise to our true Divine nature. I strive daily to have oneness with God in my thoughts, action and emotions. It is the acceptance of God's love, grace, and forgiveness that set us free. According to the Bhagavad Gita, "Man is made by his belief. As he believes, so he is," and I am finding this to be very true.

When we meditate, we surrender our senses, thoughts and any negative beliefs. We just become one with our source and embrace the Divine love that is within and without. Meditation helps me see more clearly the path to truth and it helps me dispel negative thinking and beliefs. The closer I get to the fullness of the light from meditation, the more of my former beliefs begin to change. Meditation done regularly leads to pureness of mind. Pureness of mind happens when negative and false beliefs are relinquished.

11. Awareness of Divinity (Within and Without)

When I was young, I was fascinated by nature. I still am, actually. Nature, to me, feels peaceful and comforting. I would feast my eyes on the parade of clouds, flight of the birds, and all the different insects and creatures around my apartment complex, school, and even tried to raise some as pets like lady bugs, spiders, planarian, water daphnia, salamanders, praying mantis, etc. While in the park, I would lift up stones only to be surprised by various insects as they were resting like earwigs, Jerusalem crickets, or sow bugs. What I was doing at my early age was connecting with Divinity as I marveled at all of God's creation. In college, I remember looking through a microscope at a blood vessel. I could see the cells moving through it and thought it looked like cars on the freeway. I thought it was so beautiful and Divine.

The Divine is everywhere, even where we least expect it. The book, *Autobiography of a Yogi*, sheds light on the Divinity that exists even in a plant. It is a fascinating story of an enlightened spiritual Guru whom I truly admire. In the book, Yogananda meets a professor, Jagadis Chandra Bose, who is a physicists, botanist, and inventor of the Cresco graph. The Cresco graph is a device for measuring growth in plants. The professor used it to detect a fern's perception of pain and stimulus placed on it and Yoganada wrote about his experience witnessing this:

My gaze was fixed eagerly on the screen which reflected the magnified fern-shadow. Minute life-movements were now clearly perceptible; the plant was growing very slowly before my fascinated eyes. The scientist touched the tip of the fern with a small metal bar. The developing pantomime came to an abrupt halt, resuming its' eloquent rhythms as soon as the rod was withdrawn. My companion (here in the role of a villain) thrust a sharp instrument through a part of the fern; pain was indicated by spasmodic flutters. When he passed a razor partially through the stem, the shadow was violently agitated, then stilled itself with the final punctuation of death.

When we look at the universe within and without, we see how everything is so precise, mathematical, and Divine. The synapses in between our neurons allow us to think, move, and create. Our body is going through millions of chemical reactions every day and it is amazing we don't have a system failure with all the things that can go wrong if the timing is off by even a little. What is true within is also true without. In Dr. Deepak Chopra's audio CD, *Life After Death: The Burden of Proof*, he talked about Irwin Laslow, a prominent writer on science and consciousness:

According to Laslow and other systems analyst physics had hit a wall; it couldn't explain how the universe managed to be so precisely coordinated... The big bang, which contains so much energy in a space million times smaller than an atom and millions of galaxies still express only four percent of it, occurred within a tiny window of possibility. If the expanding universe moving at millions of miles per minute had been off by a fraction of a second, the formation of stars and galaxies would have been impossible because the momentum of the explosion would have exceeded the ability of gravity, the weakest force of nature to halt it. Only the most delicate balancing act kept the push pull of two forces so close together that they can dance together instead of tearing each other apart.

This perfect dance that Laslow writes about gave birth to everything in the universe including us as well. We just lose that perfection through our beliefs, perceptions and living away from the Divine. When we are one with our source, God, or Divinity, we are in alignment with our perfection again.

The perfection of the universe within and without expresses itself through mathematical beauty and even in music. I believe music that motivates and inspires get their inspiration from Divinity like music from Puccini, Erik Satie, Debussy, Bach, Handel, Chopin, etc. My favorite is a piece from Samuel Barber's *Adagio for Strings, op 17* which I feel is one of the most Divine pieces I have ever heard. Earlier we discussed how Dr. Emoto discovered how Divinity was even in water. It is quite interesting and amazing the research Dr. Emoto did with water. However, what he also discovered in his research was that when he exposed classical music to (in my opinion, the music of the universe) water and froze it, it formed perfect and beautiful crystals. Conversely, when Dr. Emoto exposed water to heavy metal music, deformed crystals formed when it was frozen.

For thousands of years, people have tried to define and locate the human soul. I see the soul like a raindrop. When it rains each raindrop is like a soul descending to mother earth from the Heavens. The distance from the clouds to mother earth represents life's journey. Some go through life with a sense of heaviness; some go through life lightly. Others are more divine and spiritual during their existence like snowflakes. Others have an ice hard soul that pushes and hurts those in the way like hail.

Perhaps we go through life with a certain manifestation but unlike rain we can always choose to change how we go through life through divine intervention. At the end of life's journey, the raindrops collect as water which goes to the ground, into plants, fields, ditches, rivers, streams, and becomes one with them. It nourishes mother earth. Eventually, our raindrops join together and change forms. The Divine gives birth or new life to us as we evaporate and transition back up from whence we came and join up as part of a cloud of Divinity or beyond. It's like T.S. Elliot once said, "We shall not cease from exploration, and the end of all our exploring will be to arrive where we started and know the place for the first time."

Most cultures have their own religion, beliefs, about the Divine and the soul. Many insist that theirs is the ultimate truth and all others are wrong. I sincerely believe that there is one Divinity or truth with many manifestations. The sunlight represents the one truth and the rainbow to me represents the message that truth is made of different spectrums, colors and manifestations. I had an epiphany when looking at it. I believe everything in the universe is intelligent, interconnected, and correlated. If the message is Divine, we may find a similar message within our own body universe. Like our Chakras. It is the rainbow in our body. It is very interesting to note that the entire color spectrum in the rainbow is exactly the same as in our chakra and even in the same sequence from red, orange, yellow, green, blue or indigo and violet. I do not believe anything in the universe is coincidental.

The gift of Divinity is free to all. Divinity is like a membership discount. When you have a membership at a store, you get to receive the benefits of certain sales or discounts. All you have to do to become a member is fill out a form. And once it is completed, the individual gets to have the benefits of members discount right away. Divinity is in all of us. It is implied that all can have membership to Divinity. It just takes acceptance of the free gift. Instead of filling out an application, an individual must simply accept that Divinity is within them, live a spiritual life, and go on the quest to search for it.

As I become more spiritual, I look forward to living a more simplistic life. Henry David Thoreau once said, "Simplify, simplify, and simplify." The simpler our lives are, the closer we are to Divinity. When I became successful in the material world, I lost myself. The more of the material world I give up, the more my life becomes Divine and I become more awake and begin to really live following the Divine navigation guide within. How do we get there? Dr. Wayne Dyer says, "When you succeed in connecting your energy with the divine realm through higher awareness and the practice of undiscriminating virtue, the transmission of the ultimate subtle truths will follow." I think that the subtle truths manifest in our dreams, meditation, as well as in our intuition. Oneness with God gives us the guidance we need for life.

12. Control Over Emotions

Most of my life, my emotions were like a roller coaster ride and I just held on tight as I went through the twists and turns. I never thought I could get a handle on my emotions. Emotions were just like storm clouds, you hope they pass quickly but while the rain falls you grab an umbrella and hope it stops soon. Sometimes the emotional storm can be so turbulent and last so long and cause so much damage to those around you. Then as I learned how to take more control of my mind, I realized that all my feelings and thought processes, whether positive or negative were really a conscious choice I had made. It is true that our subconscious affects how we feel but, ultimately, we choose how our mind's climate will be. Joel Osteen once said in his audio CD, *Living in Favor, Abundance, and Joy*, "You can choose what kind of day you are going to have; we can choose how we are going to live our lives."

When negative emotions rise, I start to count my blessings. Then I smile. Joel Osteen suggests, "If we want to rise above our emotions, you have to learn to smile by faith. We have to put a smile on our face first then the joy will come." I put on a huge smile on my face. At first, I thought this was ridiculous. My mouth was smiling but my heart and eyes were frowning. I would laugh at how silly I looked and that was enough to make me feel better. Other times, I would imagine myself doing something fun then I begin to feel better. Or I would incorporate deep breathing for several minutes or longer until my emotions shift. Sometimes I listened to inspirational music. With practice, I got better at managing my thoughts and emotions. This has helped me to achieve greater peace, giving me joy in all my relationships and all that I do.

What I have learned now is that negative emotions and thinking is natural in this material world. We have it but it doesn't have to define who we are and how we go about our lives. I have lived my life on auto-pilot so I was ruled by negative thinking and emotions. However, now I realize that they are creations of my mind and hence can be altered by my mind through conscious awareness, choice, and practice. Sometimes use of affirmations or other positive words or phrases can be helpful to shift our moods.

"Keep calm and carry on," are great words to live by. I also love, "Hang loose." The calmer our mind is, the more focused and efficient we become. It is also easier to follow our Divine navigation guide when there are minimum conflicts in our mind.

13. Prayer

Prayer is powerful. Studies show that prayer results in physical and mental transformation. A scientific study conducted at San Francisco General Hospital's Coronary Care Unit in 1982-83 on the effects of prayer found that patients who received prayer were healthier than those who had not. The patients who had been prayed for had less need for CPR, ventilators, and antibiotics—and there were fewer deaths in those patients.[3] Another study by Dr. Franklin Loehr showed how prayer affected germinating seeds where they were done. Prayer helped speed germination and produced more healthy plants whereas when negative prayers were given to seeds it actually halted germination in some plants.[4]

Sometimes in the hustle and bustle of life we lose sense of how to deal with things. I believe that prayer should be a part of our daily routine and that we should pray with gratitude and supplication to the life that God gives each one of us. We should pray and count our many blessings. We should pray for others, the world at large, and ourselves. When things are drastic, I believe prayers need to be more focused and intense. Praying with conviction and even visualize the outcome of what we pray to manifest and amplify the Divinity within the situation.

Prayer is one way in which we connect with one another through space and time. Never doubt the power of prayer. Pray before any important event whether good or bad to help yourself stay connected to Divinity. I always prayed for the health of my loved ones and my business. I pray before I make any major decisions in life. I pray for my family, friends and those I meet along life's path. Prayer has united my wife and I and it is my dream that my children will one day discover the power of prayer. Dr. Wayne Dyer tells us that when we pray, we are talking to God and he replies through our intuition.

14. Passion

One of the key principles of success is living a life of passion. We must find passion with what we do for it is through that that we truly manifest the Divinity within. Finding what we were called to do may take a lifetime to discover. Some find it early on. We all find it by aligning ourselves with the Divine. The sooner we do that, the sooner we discover what we are called to do.

We all have a different calling in life. Some will be leaders, doctors, therapists, teachers, artists, musicians, priests, spiritual guides, while others may be mothers, fathers, gardeners, farmers, salespeople, baristas, hairstylists, fashion designers, etc. Do whatever makes you feel joy, and do it the best that you can. Not everyone is going to be Gandhi, Abraham Lincoln, or Martin Luther King, Jr. Just do what you love. The awards, accolades, and fame don't matter.

My son ran cross-country in high school. Everyone on the team wanted to be the best and place in the highest level at the end of each event. However, there were only six spots that received a medal. My son's coach, Bob, taught the kids to do their own personal best. He would recognize those who may have not been a great runner but had a significant improvement in his personal score. What the team learned was to be the best they can be, and not be so concerned about competing with someone else.

I see so many people who are burnt out. They are just going through life like hamsters on a wheel. No passion at all. How do we find our passion? Sometimes it is right in front of us but we let issues get in the way and block us from seeing it. If we are not happy with what we are doing, we must find what drives us to receive joy from within our lives. At one point I was burnt out from my work and career taking on too much overtime, letting stress get the best out of me. My ego was also in control then. I would take things personally on how people would react to me. I was more concerned about how people felt about what I did and became anxious, nervous and stressed out.

Then I reconnected to the passion I once had in helping people heal. My joy is in identifying the problems and issues affecting the client. I am like a detective looking for clues to discover the ultimate reason behind their particular illness or impediment. Once I evaluate my clients, I create a plan for helping them regain back as much functional independence as possible. I see the client as a holistic human being with psychological, emotional, spiritual and social needs. Sometimes the impairment is so severe that it seems like nothing can be done but if I allow my creative mind to work, I can find some way to help the client achieve some goal that is important to them. I once had a client who wasn't able to do anything—he was unable to move his body or limbs at all. All he could do was move his head. After some thinking, I decided that I would capitalize on what he was able to do so I got him a mouth wand which enabled him to draw or paint. He was so happy with just this because it was the first time in a very long while that he was able to do anything.

My most challenging group of patients are those who have suffered from a stroke. I find it so exciting to help unravel the blockages from my clients preventing them from getting motor movements or control. I teach my clients exercises to help them integrate abnormal reflex patterns affecting movement. I work on soft tissue mobilization, acupressure, energetic work, and exercises to improve brain and limb connections. I use both eastern and western techniques to bring out the best in my clients. It is the most rewarding thing for me to see a person who has no movements move again.

Sometimes when we go with the natural flow of life and seek to be one with God, we find our dharma. Dharma is a Sanskrit word that means law but when I use it here it takes on another meaning which is the natural order present in the universe. It refers to all behaviors considered correct, appropriate or morally upright encompassing such notions as duty, vocation, and religion. In other words, we do what we are destined and meant to do.

As I started to evolve more spiritually and started to write this book, I discovered that I had a passion for writing. I could write all day long so absorbed in what I am writing about that I forget any worries or concerns in life. Therefore, we should always, "Seek ye first the kingdom of God, and his righteousness; and all these things shall be added unto you." (Matthew 6:33). Be one with God and you will be guided to where you should be in life. Where you should be is where your passion is.

Kina Grannis won a video competition that was aired during Super Bowl. She was offered a record deal but turned it down to be able to stay pure and creative with her music. She went on to release two CDs. She tours all over the U.S. as well as abroad. I was fortunate to have seen her perform live in San Francisco and meet her afterwards. She is a great musician and artist. She truly loves what she does and the people who support her. She has a huge fan base all over the world. She is passionate with her music and strives hard to produce great music and connect with her audience and fans. Kina is quite passionate with her music and really connects with her audience. Many people admire and love her music.

Suguru Kurosawa is another person who has turned his love of reading children's stories to a theatrical level. I met him about five years ago in Tokyo. We became instant friends. When he reads, he gets in into character using voices, singing, and gestures. He captures the complete attention of his audiences—both children and adults. His performances are very entertaining. He has even made a name for himself in Tokyo and performs frequently for the Japanese community in San Jose, San Francisco and elsewhere. He sings, dances, plays the ukulele and also is a writer- he has published one book and is on his second. He truly enjoys what he does and is outstanding at doing it.

My wife, Cassandra, is passionate in her career as a clinical nurse consultant for a large company that provides consultation services to skilled nursing facilities throughout California. She gets into an organization in total chaos, dissects issues, and comes up with the appropriate action plan to turn a failing facility into a stellar health care operation. She also knows a great deal about health care law in long-term care facilities. Through her work, facilities systems are developed to improve safety, quality of care, and dignity of life of all residents at the facilities where she consults. What I have noticed is that the tougher the situation at work, the more she seems to thrive. She seems to thrive on chaos. I really admire her passion in her job. If my wife were an advisor on Obama's healthcare initiative, I know she would be able to devise a comprehensive plan that would be great for all of us. She is really that good.

I recently met the most fascinating person I have met in a while. He is an extraordinary man who has such a diverse background, from a corporate consultant, businessman, Qi Gong healer, writer, calligrapher, and basketball coach. He is very religious and serves God in all he does. He currently owns a very discreet and modest flower shop in Chinatown. In fact, I never knew it existed until my mom, out of the blue, just wanted to buy plants for her apartment. As my wife and I slowly walked down the stairs to this hidden flower shop, we had no idea what to expect. We talked a little to the florist and he just opened up the world to us.

We were so impressed with his positive energy, passion and love for what he does. He is very happy with what he is doing and was very passionate in telling us about how his shop was selected to make the bouquet for the 2008 Olympics as they carried the torch to San Francisco. I found him quite intriguing as he goes on to tell me how he selected all the floral arrangements and all the symbolism that were in the arrangements he put together. He spoke with such conviction and passion it was amazing. He really enjoyed what he did. He even talked about how he liked the Qi of his plants. He has been offered jobs but chose to do this business because he truly enjoys it and loves to share his love and passion to people. We left his store feeling energized and happy.

What all these people have in common is the passion for what they do. They love doing what they do, are good at it, and because of that they bring happiness and joy to others. They are not motivated by money or awards but are simply happy to share their passion with others.

15. Gratitude

Our society teaches that happiness comes from material things, attainment of a certain body shape or type (no matter how emaciated it may be), going to a certain college, or having a certain job. If you think about it, only a small minority can achieve those ideals if ever. The majority of us spend our lives trying to measure up and feel inadequate because we don't have those traits or material things.

Even the people who have all these things realize that they still are not happy. It never ceases to amaze me how people who seem to have it all—fame and fortune—but are still unhappy. We hear about rich and famous people all the time coping with life through alcohol, drugs, etc. Something is definitely wrong and the world is crying out for help, yet many people are doing so in negative or unproductive ways.

Meanwhile, many people are depressed or unhappy trying to be something they are not, or have things they cannot afford. If we can learn to change our perspective and give thanks for what we have, we begin to become free of this materialistic world. Perhaps those who are rich, should be thankful they have what they have and that they are in a good position to make a big difference in many lives through their resources of talent and finances. There is always something to be thankful for no matter how hopeless things may appear. Joel Osteen talks about how we can get out of depression by giving gratitude for all the blessings in our lives.

I am grateful for all my blessings-for my health, my family, my wonderful children, my mother's health, my business, my friends, and my ability to help and facilitate the healing process of people. As I think about all these blessings, sadness starts to dissipate and float away. I see some of the most heart-wrenching cases in my work. I feel compassion for them and give thanks for what I have. I see clients sometimes who can't walk, talk, eat, move, or even think. As I drive through many cities, I see people who still eat from the garbage can and sleep on the streets. We should be thankful we have a bed to sleep, a home to stay in, a car to drive, or a bus to ride, a church to pray in, a mouth to sing and talk, legs to bring us around or dance, and a mind to imagine and create. I pray and give gratitude daily before I meditate and start my day. I give gratitude anytime negative thoughts seep in. Rumi says, "Wear gratitude like a cloak and it will feed every corner of your life."

My mother taught me to love music, dancing (she was a ballroom dancer), nature, and fashion. She taught me how to be street smart and how to live life as a prince or a pauper. Essentially, she told me that it wasn't the material things that defined happiness. Although it is nice to have it, we can learn to be happy without it by giving to others of our time and love. She has taught me many good principles to live by which are based on Confucius teachings. She taught me how to have respect for the elders and the importance of family. She later taught me the importance of giving of your time, money and service. I am grateful to her for all these things.

My father allowed me to find my own path in life. I am thankful that he supported me financially through school. I am grateful that he opened up to me in his last few years of life. Although my father didn't say a whole lot most of his life, I somehow internalized his dreams or visions just by seeing what he liked in his room—from the poem, *Press On*, to the lyrics of his favorite song, *The Impossible Dream*, to the interesting Golden Rule ball he had in his drawer. They all served as subliminal principles that have helped me to become the person I am today.

We can choose to hold on to the wrongs that were done or we can choose to remember the good things we have learned. Everything happens for a reason. It is up to us to discover it and be free through forgiveness and gratitude. I have deep gratitude for my life and pray daily that I can give back each day to all those I come in contact as much as possible. As I have more gratitude in my life, I began to experience a greater level of peace and serenity within. To be truly grateful is to be truly divine.

About two years ago, I called my doctor, Dr. Sidney Goodman, to schedule a visit because I felt emotionally distraught. He was extremely busy but because I was so desperate, he was willing to compromise his lunch break to accommodate me. As he arrived to our appointment, he asked if I had eaten and I stated that I did not. He offered me half of his sandwich without hesitation. He always treated me with dignity and respect, being a true example of "humanity" in medicine.

His care and gentle approach I think contributed to my healing in all aspects. I never forgot his kindness and his caring heart. Two years later, I returned for a belated impromptu visit. I went and bought him his favorite sandwich and a latte to show him my gratitude for all he had done for me. I told him how well I was doing and that I truly wanted to thank him for all the help he gave me in facilitating my healing. He was taken aback by my transformation and said I had transformed like a lotus. When I first saw him, I was depressed, anxious, and completely stressed out. I had an extremely low self-esteem. He later emailed me telling me how impressed he was with my "quantum leap" in transformation. It is important that we tell everyone how thankful we are to those that have impacted our lives in a positive way.

I wrote earlier about Dr. Emoto's research with water. Although the word love written on a glass of water created a beautiful crystal; he discovered that when the words gratitude and love were written on a Petri dish or cup of water and the water was frozen, the crystals formed were even more beautiful and had more depth to it. I believe love and gratitude are two of the most important spiritual principles that should motivate our every action.

16. Oneness with Divinity

The ultimate gateway towards oneness with Divinity is meditation. I have discussed meditation throughout this book but in this section, I will dive deeper into the practice and its benefits. Meditation has been practiced for centuries in many civilizations including Tibet, China, Egypt, India, Japan, and other European countries. Meditation is an important part of Sufi tradition of Islam and the Kabbalistic tradition of Judaism. The early priests, Reishis, Saints, and Mystics and other spiritual beings around the world used it as a means to connect with Divinity.

Father Kevin Joyce, Ph.D., Catholic Priest, and founder and executive director of Spirit Site, the Catholic Spirituality Center for the Diocese of San Jose, gave a lecture on April 27, 2008 entitled, Eastern Meditation and Christian Contemplation Compared. He stated that every recognized saint in the first 1,500 years of Christianity, both Eastern and Western Saints had practiced some form of meditation.

Early Catholic teachings included monastic prayer and meditations. The Church never lost the meditation tradition. It was kept alive especially in monasteries, convents, and religious orders that engaged in active ministry in the world, such as the Jesuits, Franciscans, and Dominicans. Some saints put great emphasis on lay people practicing meditation.

In the same lecture Father Joyce talked about a letter written by Cardinal Joseph Ratzinger (later Pope Benedict XVI) on meditation[5]:

> *Just as the Catholic Church rejects nothing of what is true and holy in these non-Christian religions. Neither should these meditation practices be rejected out of hand simply because they are not Christian. On the contrary, one can take from them what is useful so long is the Christian conception of prayer, its' logic and requirements are never obscured. Genuine practices of meditation which comes from the Christian East and from the great non-Christian religions, which prove attractive to the person of today who is divided and disoriented, can constitute a suitable means of helping the person who prays to come before God with an interior peace, even in the midst of external pressures.*

Father Joyce goes on to discuss the importance of meditation for self-realization but to do it to have union with God. He stated he was shocked how many meditators he had met who have been doing it for over 20 years had no conscious awareness and relationship with God. He encourages meditators of other faiths to just accept Jesus' invitation. Father Joyce also talked about how Maharishi Mahesh Yogi knows that a person can remain satisfied with self-realization and fail to reach God unless he or she receives knowledge about God. He stressed how we need to open up to God's self-revelation by means of a life of prayer, devotion to God, worship of God, service of people, and in context of a community.

Meditation is the ultimate gateway to connecting with Divinity. All holy spiritual books talk about it as a mean to reach oneness. It is the only time we are truly one with Divinity. If we live a life of gratitude, service, love, compassion, integrity, and prayer, we will soon discover the Divinity within. With the help of a spiritual guide, we may one day have an interactive and Divine experience which will only deepen our peace, love and happiness and will only catapult us to a new level of reality.

The great Indian saint, Yogananda, had this conscious awareness and relationship with God as well as many other Saints, Mystics and people who are on the Spiritual path. According to Yogananda, "He who is persistent will realize God. So try your best to make meditation a regular experience in your life." I wish and pray that churches and other groups will begin to bring back meditation as a spiritual tool to get closer to God.

Before I meditate, I wash my hands and drink water to prepare for the purity of myself to connect with Divinity. I prepare my meditation shrine by lighting two candles and an incense. I then sit in Lotus position and I take a small dowel and circle around my Tibetan Singing bowl until it gives out a rich, deep tone that brings peace and clarity to the space around me in the early morning hours. I proceed to pray and give thanks to God for my life, health, my family, friends, work and the world. I pray for others who are in need or despair. I then visualize myself being surrounded by a white light for protection (a technique I learned from Averi Torres to prepare me for meditation).

I do three deep cleansing breaths then I visualize going up each one of my seven chakras invoking words of affirmation, Divinity and words relevant to Chakra balancing. Thereafter, I do three deep cleansing breaths and begin to chant mantras for some time then proceed to "stillness" with body, mind and spirit as long as I can while I am being one with God and the universe. During the meditation process, I direct my energy and thoughts toward the point between and above my eyebrow. To many, it is known as the third eye point. When I am done with chanting, I drift into a stillness and allow myself to be one with the universe and God. When I am done with being in stillness, I continue to have conscious awareness of God and pray to him throughout the day for support and guidance. There are many different forms of meditation: I am-Integrated Amrita, Zen, TM, Kriya Yoga, Chakra, Lectio Divina, Fa Lun Dafa, Hong Sau, etc.

Some people find it easier to follow a meditation CD which may be a good way to get started but evolving further from that is the goal. Dr. Wayne Dyer has various meditation CDs that are very helpful as well. Self-Realization Fellowship (SRF) and Amma's organization offer meditation training as well. What is important is we find the one that resonates well with us and allows us to have clearness of mind.

Meditation, in my opinion, should be taught to everyone whether you are on a spiritual quest or just want to manifest more in life or just want to be healthy. Amma says that meditation elevates the soul from the body, mind, and intellect to absolute peace and bliss. Amma offers meditation training to all who are willing to learn. Amma stated, "Spiritual knowledge is the birthright of humankind." In fact, she offers free training. She stated, "To charge for meditation classes is like charging a baby for breast milk."

Meditation at the basic level is great for stress reduction, improving mental clarity and improving basic health. It is useful for everyone from students, CEOs, workers, athletes, actors, and senior citizens. MIT and Harvard researchers have completed a study on the effects of meditation on chronic pain and noted that it was helpful.[6] In a blog post on the website, Food Matters TV, the author lists seven benefits of deep relaxation or meditation:[7]

- Increased immunity.
- Emotional balance.
- Increased fertility.
- Relieves irritable bowel syndrome.
- Lowers blood pressure.
- Anti-inflammatory.
- Calmness.

I met a professor who is also meditator. She shared with me that research has shown that it has helped test scores of students. For me, it has helped me to achieve calmness in life, enriched and mature my spiritual experiences and brings me closer to God.

Here are some simple techniques I have found very helpful to get you started on your own meditation practice. First, you might want to set up a simple meditation shrine that might include pictures or statues of religious or spiritual figures on a small table for inspiration. I like to use white candles to represent purity. You can choose to burn incense too if that suits you. I also like to use a Tibetan Singing bowl to help me create the mood, energy and vibration conducive to meditation. Then you can do the following:

- Wear something comfortable and loose fitting.
- Find a nice quiet place to meditate.
- Sit with your back straight with your legs crossed.
- Your chin should be parallel to the floor.
- Focus your thought and attention to the point above and between your eye brows.
- For those with knee problems, sit on a comfortable chair. Sit towards the edge of the chair and have body slightly leaning forward but back is still erect.

- Rest your arms on your lap. You can choose to have your thumb and index fingers touch with the palm faced up. This is also called a mudra in the lotus position. Some say it can help generate knowledge, wisdom, receptivity and calmness. Keep in mind that there are many different hand positions depending on which technique you choose.[8] I recommend a prayer of gratitude before you start. You can also pray that God guides you in your meditation and be there with you as you seek him and his love. Remember ask and it will be given to you, seek and you shall find. Since meditation is the gateway and the path to God, you can rest assured that he is in even closer proximity and quite ready to reach out and help you.
- Visualize yourself surrounded by the white light of God.
- Focus your thoughts inwards and breath in and out slowly. Begin by breathing slowly in through your nose for four seconds, hold for the same time, then slowly exhale with pursed lips the same time.
- You may want to chant a mantra to help you focus inwards and slowly relinquishing all thoughts and feelings. A basic mantra you can chant is "OM." Others may feel more comfortable reading a passage from the bible or other Holy book that inspires you to feel the grace and love of God prior to meditation. Once you have that spiritual feeling bring it into meditation as you focus on your breathing and communion and oneness with God. Regardless of which approach you choose, the important thing is to allow thoughts to slowly drift away to allow you to have stillness of body and mind. As you reach the stillness phase, allow yourself to slowly breathe in and out of the nose

until you reach complete stillness. Stay there as long as you can.

- As thoughts come, tell them to go away by saying, "Peace be still." Or command it to settle down or be silent for you are in the presence of Divinity. Do what you need to do to let your thoughts flow away leading into your stillness.

- To finish the meditation, you can raise your hand and give thanks to God or you may put your hands together in prayer position and bow forward to give respect to God.

It is not important how you are doing it when you get started. It is more important that you do it daily (especially in the early morning if possible; if not whenever you have some quiet time), and do it with a pure heart. Don't do it to search for something Divine to happen. Just allow the process to manifest itself to you when you are ready. Do it because you are thirsty for God's unconditional love. When you do that, pray daily, live a life full of love, compassion and forgiveness, God will guide you on how to get closer to him.

There is so much more to help you go deeper but I have just given you the most basic tools to get you started on the right track. Once you get the swing of it and want to go deeper, start looking for a technique which resonates with you; then find a mentor, center, teacher, guide, or guru to help you connect further into higher consciousness. When you first start to meditate you can do it initially at five minutes, 10 minutes, and work your way up to 20 minutes or more.

May your first meditation be filled with peace and serenity. May this seed you plant continue to grow until it helps you to find God and your ultimate peace, love, and happiness.

17. Press On

This is one of the most important principles of manifesting our goal or dream. Perseverance makes up for our flaws in life. If we are determined to achieving our goal, we will one day get there. Nothing can replace hard work and persistence. Many a times I wanted to quit in life because I felt like a failure. I didn't do too well in Chinese school, wasn't the smartest kid, didn't have much support in life, wasn't very socially adroit, wasn't a good speaker, was extremely shy, was extremely negative, and had an extremely low self-esteem. However, who would have guessed that funny poem my dad had posted on his room entitled, *Press On*, would plant a seed in my heart to help me be a guiding principle in life.

I remember watching my brother teach my sister how to ride the bike. I watched how she struggled, how she lost her balance and what worked for her. I grabbed my bike and tried it myself. I had trouble getting on the bike at first because it was too high for me. Next I had to figure out how to keep my balance and keep the bike moving. I used the principle of motion for a scooter to get the motion going then remembered how my sister got the bike moving by pedaling so once I got moving I started pedaling and soon I had mastered it all by myself. Of course I made a lot of mistakes learning how to ride a bike but that is all part of the process. I held onto the feeling that I could do this if I kept at it. I kept getting up each time I fell. I just decided I wasn't going to give up until I had mastered it.

I had that same experience when I was going through my internship at Kentfield Rehab Hospital many years ago. I was a frustrated trying to get a grasp of all these new things I was learning. I just told myself that I wasn't going to give up, no matter how long it took me. Consequently, I was able to have a successful internship.

When I ventured into the real world, there were many times when I wanted to take the easy way out. I wanted to quit and just get an easy job. My clients were too complex or the staff was too political. I cried many times early on and just wanted to go back to school or change careers. Fortunately, my wife, friends and colleagues were very supportive and encouraged me to hang in there. My mom would remind me of the Chinese adage which translated into English means, "The more you fail and learn from it, the more you will succeed." Those were comforting words that I needed to keep me going. I just kept going forward every time I fell but chanted my mom's words and prayed to God for help.

I became quite effective as a clinician and became a mentor and resource person for many of my colleagues. If I gave up early on I would not have achieved my past and current levels of success. Where I am today is a culmination of the many years of hard work, sweat, tears, and my will to keep moving forward despite wanting to give up. Life is not easy but if we remain true to ourselves and persevere in being the best at what we can do, success will always follow us wherever we may go.

During my spiritual journey, many issues would come up that would try to derail me. The spiritual path is not an easy one and takes a lot of dedication and commitment. Every step of the way is full of obstacles and challenges. As I got more spiritual, I soon realized that the flip side of problems is opportunities for learning and growth. Many times, I just wanted to cling on to my old comfortable predictable life. It takes a lot of mental and emotional energy to stay on the spiritual path. Many times I just wanted to quit and just live a normal life. However, I am glad I didn't. I now see the world and reality in a whole new way. The result is that I have transformed as a person and have found real success, happiness, and peace within.

18. Compassion

Compassion means stepping outside of your own concerns and being sympathetic to others. When we live without compassion, we live a life that is ego driven. As we know by now, that kind of life rarely leads to true happiness and success. When we live without compassion, it is like living with blinders on—we are living in a delusion that we are the only ones who matter in this world. Without compassion, our civilization would just wither away from all the greed. The act of compassion helps us to evolve. When we have compassion, we think beyond ourselves and activate the love in our heart. When we do that, we grow, mature, and awaken. Compassion requires love, understanding, empathy, and gives birth to service. There are so many people who are in dire need of help. We can offer our talents, time, resources, or even prayer. We can all have compassion in our own way.

When I was focused on material success, I was concerned with my goals and ambitions. I was not concerned about others. I was always on the run and not living in the moment. I started to burn out rather quickly. However, once I slowed down and reevaluated my life and purpose, I realized that I had to change my attitude or changed what I did. I decided to change the way I felt and thought. I remember a saying from Confucius, "Choose a job you love and you will never have to work a day of your life."

After I changed my way of thinking, I was interested in learning about clients as human beings rather than something I needed to fix. I realized that I was dealing with people who really needed my services and that I had tools that could make a difference in their lives. I found myself joking with patients and we would have such a fun time laughing together. I started to get creative about how I could make a difference one client at a time. The more compassion I had for my clients, the better they responded.

Recently, a client of mine told me that her walker brakes were broken as well as her showerhead. I didn't know how to repair it so I told her she had to contact the medical company where she bought the walker from to repair it. I further told her she had to have her family or friends help replace the shower head. Unfortunately, she didn't have any help or support available. That evening I meditated and received a message that I needed to go beyond what I was doing for my client. I usually don't go out of my way to help my clients beyond the rehabilitation services but realized that Divinity was prompting me to be more compassionate.

I quickly went online to research how to repair my client's rollator walker and discovered how to fix it on YouTube. The next day I decided to drop by on my day off to help my client with her repairs. I tried fixing the shower head but it was broken beyond repair. I later went and bought a new shower head and replaced the old one. My client was so elated by what I had done. Seeing her smile, the glow in her face, and the happiness she felt made my day. She was deeply touched and had the utmost gratitude for what I had done. That moment was priceless.

I now realize sometimes we just have to give our time, money, skill and help to those in need because it can truly make a huge difference. Once I was having dinner with my friend, Paul, at a restaurant in San Francisco. I noticed an elderly woman standing outside the restaurant. I had a window seat so she was close to where I was sitting. She gestured to the bread we had on our table. I went ahead and ordered a whole loaf of fresh bread and gave it to her discreetly. After she received the bread, I thought she left. A short while later, the old woman returned and stood in front of the window and had a glow of deep appreciation.

She looked at me and gestured her gratitude. I acknowledged her and just smiled. It gave me great joy to make a difference for this one lady.

I had no idea how my transformation would extend to all of God's creation. As a child and most of my adult life, I would have no hesitation to swat a fly, stomp on a bug, or smash an ant. However, now, I find it difficult to harm even the smallest of God's creatures. I noticed a fly in my house a few months ago. I looked at it with compassion. I sought a way to guide it back outside. So far I have been fortunate to find a way to guide them back out. My family looked at me oddly. As I am writing this book, an ant comes towards me. Typically, I would crush it but I paused and relocated it but then five minutes later, it was back on my table toward me as if to challenge me. I again relocated it further away. Again, 15 minutes later it approached me again. Finally I scooped him up and brought him to the backyard where he belonged. That was the last time I saw him. Such a small creature but making a big point. What I learn from this ant is to have a new perspective that all of God's creation great and small is special. If I can give it a chance to live, I would be spreading love and compassion in my own little way.

CHAPTER 7

Supporting Your Temple

Since we are Divine beings in a physical body we have to take care of our temple. What we take in our mind and body does have some effect on our overall spiritual, emotional, and physical well-being. The better we feel, the easier we are able to find peace and happiness.

Once again, I am not a licensed physician and anything you do you need to check with your doctor. I am simply sharing what I did on my road to health with the hope that you might learn for yourself the relationship between our body, mind, spirit, and nutrition. Those seeking actual comprehensive knowledge with nutrition should consult their physician and nutritionist. I only talk about nutrition in terms of spiritualism and general terms because I feel it has relevance to our happiness and oneness with Divinity.

Supplements and Holistic Herbs

During the first seven years of my marriage, my health was not good. I was sick at least three to five times a year with colds and flus. I also started to develop severe rash on my back that seemed to grow worse with the stressors in life. At the time, I didn't see the correlation. I was also dealing with depression. I started to read up on natural means to help improve my health and discovered *Spontaneous Healing,* by Dr. Andrew Weil. He talked about all types of methods and alternative and holistic healing methods. I also purchased *An Encyclopedia of Alternative Medicine* and used it as a reference guide.

I started to taking a natural herb called St. John's Wort and felt better. That sparked my interest in taking herbs, vitamins, and homeopathic supplements. For the next decade, I went on a quest to find all those supplements that were good for my body. Soon I had amassed over a dozen different types of supplements. I had a supplement for every problem that came up, my health and immune system did improve by all this and soon I was sharing my supplements to my family as well. My wife would always joke about how many herbs I would take. She would say how I would outlive all the family and relatives and I would be alone one day or I would choke from taking too many vitamins.

However, I would continue taking my supplements because I would continue to see benefits. I would take Co-enzyme Q10, fish oil, flax seed, colon cleanser, multiple vitamin, etc. Then if I felt something like a cold coming on I would take a tincture of Standardized Echinacea with some fluid or I would gargle it if I were getting a sore throat. The problem is that I started to go on an endless quest for supplement for every conceivable problem. Holistic medicine supplements are not cheap. I began to wonder about the effects of taking too much. And when is it too much?

Although the effect of holistic herbs and supplements are gentle and the side effects are less dramatic, they do have side effects. For instance, one supplement that is touted to improve memory has some side effect of thinning the blood. If you have a medical condition of hemophilia or taking aspirin, the supplement can be dangerous.

Unfortunately, the herbal market is not under the same scrutiny of the FDA. The consumer is not told this information upfront. There needs to be more information for herbs; otherwise for the most part they can be quite helpful as they were for me. However, it is very important the consumer reads up on any supplements they are taking and discuss it with their physician or health care practitioner.

Two years ago, I was talking to my wife's niece, Annabella Aquino, about what I was taking and she actually used me as her subject for her nutrition class. She felt I was taking too many supplements and that it may have an effect on my liver. That was an eye opener for me. It is true that the liver can only process so much. If I could cut back on some of the supplements, I would kill two birds with one stone: I would save money and improve my health over a greater period of time.

I eventually went to my doctor, Dr. Chang, for an annual physical exam. My doctor is extremely knowledgeable, understanding and open-minded. He is truly a great doctor and I owe my good medical health to him.

He did a comprehensive exam including cardiac exam, eye exam, blood test, and ultra sound. The results of my blood test were overall normal except that my liver readings were little high. He advised me to watch my weight to improve my liver function. I took what he said seriously and started to eat better transforming from a meat eater to more of a "flexitarian" but eventually heading toward total vegetarian diet.

Detoxification

I enrolled in a nutritional program run by a local yoga teacher and wellness coach, Umang Goel. Her center is called Umang's Wellness Haven. In the first week, I went through a process of detoxification. It was brutal but I embraced it and was able to break through many of the cravings and addictions I once had with food. During that week, I ate mostly raw vegetables. At first, I found it somewhat repulsive because things were too raw and tasteless but after a few days, I learned to acquire the taste of simplicity and finding the purity and honesty in the food that Mother Earth has provided us with.

Through eating the purity of raw fruits and vegetables, I discovered the inherent qualities of the food I was eating. I noticed the vegetable flavors and grew to enjoy them. I could taste that natural sweetness of a bell pepper, carrots, and snap peas. When I later ate fruits, it was so refreshing and the sweetness of the fruit burst out in such a delightful treat. Food in its purest form represents the natural goodness and essence of Divinity. I felt a certain level of calmness and peace in life that was deepened by this new way of eating. I began to become detached from the temptations and power food once had over me. From this detoxification experience, I soon realized that nutrition and what we put in our body does effect on our spiritual, emotional, and physical wellbeing.

This method of eating is meant to cleanse the body. The program suggests that we only detoxify once a year but I go on a modified detoxification diet to bring balance to my body, mind and spirit when I sometimes overindulge myself in family events or festivities. I may do the detox for a couple of days. When it is done, I find a sense of balance in my life again.

Umang told us to drink a glass of hot water and a half squeezed lemon to help curb our appetite and aid in the detoxification process. Susan Lee also mentioned this practice (minus the lemon) to me as a method to improve my overall health. She told me it improves circulation and oxygenation, aids in digestion, helps with constipation, and aides the body to maintain a stable central core temperature. In addition, Umang told us to slowly reintroduce proteins and more normal food into our body. After the 12-week program, I lost 17 pounds and now I am at 13 percent body fat. I feel great inside and out. I finally discovered how to eat healthy and break the power of food over me. Umang brought up how in nature animals only eat what they need. I have never seen an obese animal in the wild. There is a balance in life. We can learn a lot from nature. We need to eat to survive but must ensure to not over consume. Many people are starving around the world and we must ensure that there is enough food for generations to come and the current world population.

I cut back all unhealthy food and now eat what my body really requires. I cut back on refined sugars, processed food, fats, and carbs. The result is I feel purified, relaxed, and full of energy. I recently went to my doctor and had another complete physical including blood work including a check on my liver function. I got a clean bill of health from my doctor. All my blood work is normal including my liver function.

Eating Healthy in the Real World

It can be difficult to deal with the pressures from family and friends when we are eating out. I am not an expert in this area but have developed my own survival techniques. Coming from a Chinese family, eating banquet style is quite common. Many times we would eat a six to 10 course meal. Here are a couple of things I do that have helped me survive many big parties and banquets. I make sure I drink hot water and if possible squeeze lemon into the water to help curb the appetite before meals. Then I scan all the food to look for vegetables and I load up my plate with lots of them.

However, I have one of those mothers who insist on me trying everything and will put an assortment of food in my plate despite my protests. I will drink my cup of hot water first and maybe even another glass or two to give me some fullness then I would start to eat all my vegetables. I put no restrictions on vegetables but do put restrictions on carbohydrates. I rarely eat rice anymore, especially white rice. At one of point of my life, I stopped eating white rice all together and lost about 10 pounds without doing anything else.

If I really want rice, I request brown rice but I really try not to eat any kind of rice at all. I eat slowly and nibble things that are not healthy just to get the taste but not necessarily get all the fat. Eating slowly helps me to enjoy my meal more and also gives time for my stomach to be full.

I do my best to stay away from deep fried food or greasy food. Again, if I do happen to see my favorite fried salt and pepper spare rib I might just get one. The key thing is loading up on healthy food, drinking lots of water, and eating only small amounts of your other favorite unhealthy food. It is better to just say no to all unhealthy food but in some cases that is unrealistic.

When I was young, I was told to always to make sure I clean my plate after I ate. That was a very bad rule and habit for many years. I started to get in a habit of not finishing all my food in the past few years. If there were too much food, I would take it home for lunch or dinner the next day. When my wife and I used to dine out a lot, we would order our own meals including an appetizer. We began to realize in the past year is that most of the meals we got were enough for two people, sometimes even more. Now we order a meal and share it and maybe get one appetizer. We always order hot water, tea or iced water to fill up. We noticed that when we ate slow, drank moderate water (hot or cold) and shared a meal, we would be full enough but not stuffed.

Most of the times when I dined out, I usually order salad as a healthier option versus a pizza, burger or other greasy food. You can pretty much find salad in all restaurants nowadays. Those who are diehard healthy eaters can get vinaigrette dressing with only salad.

A friend of mine, Yumiko, told me that her father gave her some wise advice about eating. He told her to eat until she is 80 percent full. My friend and her parents are quite healthy and slim most likely through this healthy eating practice. By eating that way, we are most likely eating enough. If we eat until we are full or a little stuff, most likely we have over eaten.

Sometimes I do my best to eat healthy but find myself gaining some weight. I don't like it because my clothes get a little tighter and I don't feel as optimal as I should. I learned from Umang is that it is okay to cheat sometimes and if we fail, we just need to get back on track again. It is never the end of the world. Besides that, just having a healthy snack throughout the day can help keep the metabolism going. I typically eat six times a day (three main meals and small healthy snacks in between like nuts, fruits, or raw vegetables). Drinking lots of water is very helpful. Lastly, joining a program where there is support may be extremely helpful as I have found at the Umang's Wellness Haven. There are countless others like Weight Watchers, Nutrisystem, etc. Some people I know have consulted with their physician and had good results as well. What is important is finding the right program for a particular person's needs. If you have issues, always consult with your physician or nutritionist on which type is good for you.

When we eat, it is very important that we eat enough to help keep our colon healthy. In naturopathic medicine, it is believed that 90 percent of our problems come from issues with diet and digestion. Hence it is very important we eat properly and get enough fiber to keep our colons free flowing. If our colon is working properly, toxins and waste are eliminated and water, electrolytes and vitamins are absorbed. When that happens, we can achieve greater health. Conversely, people who eat fast food regularly and don't eat much fiber end up with constipation and may have a buildup of toxins and waste in the body, and lack of needed nutrients for the body.

What we can do for ourselves is to educate ourselves about health and be more aware of eating better and taking steps to ensure optimum physical, emotional, spiritual health. The three are intertwined. Affecting one can affect the other. As we become healthier, we minimize the load in the healthcare system for those who really need it and help extend our lives to be productive citizens to support our family and economy. Also, I believe the healthier we become, the better our body can help heal itself. Divinity works toward healing itself. However, if we abuse our bodies by not eating right and drinking excessively, it is hard for our body to heal itself. Our health is our wealth.

Cutting Back on Processed Foods

What we eat makes a difference whether we have good health or not in the long run. If we eat and drink without discretion, eventually we will start putting on excessive weight, especially if our food is high in sugar, carbohydrate, fat and sodium. Eating well can help shape the emotional and physical well-being as well. When I eat a lot of junk food, I feel irritable and sometimes depressed. Being in the medical field, I see people who have kidney failures, strokes, diabetes, heart conditions, etc. A great majority of these issues may have been avoided if they ate better and had better nutrition.

Sugar is probably one of the worst things you can eat. Though it tastes good, it wears down the immune system and makes the body susceptible to diseases like diabetes. It is a serious disease that affects many systems in our body and can cause blindness, neuropathy, or kidney failure.

Once that goes out of control it creates other problems, which increases our likelihood of getting a stroke, heart attack, and host of other problems including cancer. Dr. Wayne Dyer talks about the issues of sugar on his *Making the Shift* audio CD. Just by cutting sugar, he lost a significant amount of weight and I am sure he feels great by it and has lengthened his life. I do my best to avoid sugar and use sugar substitute but was in shock when I started to look at the side effects of it. There were many side effects including depression, anxiety, and difficulty focusing. Physical symptoms include being bloated. I quickly stopped all sugar substitutes and noticed that I was feeling better especially in the morning after coffee. Previously, I would get anxious from drinking coffee.

Not only is eating healthy important but eating quality food is even more important. I know most of the fruits we eat contain pesticides, which are not healthy and so going organic is a better bet for our health. It is better for us and healthier. However, organic food can be quite expensive. My wife is the Director of Financial Services in our family. She frequently reminds me of the "balanced budget act" she passed this year for our family expenses since we have two kids in college. I find her budget plan flawed and find it hard to follow though; I will vote to make an amendment of her bill next year. Joking aside, it is a serious issue of the price of healthy food. I only pray that quality food will one day be affordable to everyone.

Fasting

Besides eating better, I fast about once per month. It is interesting to note that as I began to fast once a month, I began to feel even more purified inside. Many religions discuss fasting including Islam, Catholicism, Buddhism and Hinduism. Great holy books like *The Bhagavad Gita* and *Hua Hu Ching* also mention about it. One doctor mentioned to me studies done on animals have showed by starving laboratory rats one or two days regularly seems to extend their lives. However, before anyone considers fasting, one should always consult your physician especially if you are of ill health or medically compromised.

People with serious illnesses, such as cancer or AIDS, should avoid fasting. Those with kidney issues, diabetes or who are on prescription medications should not fast. Infants, women who are pregnant and those who have liver problems or anemia are at risk when fasting as well.[9]

Stress Management

Stress is probably the biggest contributor to diseases and is a major block to peace and happiness. It is the biggest obstacle to anyone in any path of life, in pursuing their dreams. I have lived with it most of my life. It became the dictator of my mind universe. I was enslaved by it for many years and all my friends and family can attest to that. Eventually, I learned how to manage stress. However, it would seem to find ways of escaping and taunt me. After I studied Dr. Wayne Dyer's works, I came to realize stress is something we create ourselves. We can choose how we respond to stress.

Below is a summary of my techniques for managing stress. Some information below I added from what I have heard or read about which also may be helpful. Many and most of it, I have done or am doing currently. No matter where you are on your spiritual path, my hope is that you benefit from this information.

1. Do Something Fun or Relaxing.
   - Go to the beach.
   - Watch a funny or inspirational movie.
   - Listen to inspirational and relaxing music.
   - Do some gardening.

- Take a nature stroll in the park or lake.
- Go hiking.
- Go camping.
- Watch a musical, opera, ballet, or play.

2. Do Something Physical for 30-45 Minutes.*
   - Play Ping Pong, tennis, or other sports.
   - Take dance lessons in salsa dancing, ballroom dancing, or line dancing, etc.
   - Take a brisk walk.
   - Do yoga.
   - Do aerobics.
   - Take a Zumba class.
   - Ride a bike.
   - Go swimming.

Always consult your physician before engaging in any physical activity, especially if you are suffering any medical illness or heart conditions.

3. Meditate.
   - Meditate at least once daily 5-10 minutes initially.
   - Work your way up to 20 to 30 minutes per day.
   - Eventually it is good to do it even 30 minutes to one hour or more per day two times per day.
   - The important thing regardless of time is your sincerity and tenaciousness.
   - Doing it on a regular basis is very important.
   - Pray before you meditate and give thanks for all of your blessings.
   - Visualize yourself surrounded by the golden light of God's unconditional love while meditating.
   - Focus on the deep breathing during meditation in terms of it healing you. When you breathe in,

imagine breathing in the positive energy or the love of God and when you exhale, imagine releasing all negativity and your ego.

4. Be of Service.
 • Spend time with a family member, friend or love one that is in need.
 • Volunteer at school, senior center or in your community or church.
 • Practice random acts of kindness.

5. Get Proper Nutrition.
 • Eat and drink healthy.
 • Avoid caffeine.
 • Avoid sugar.
 • Avoid processed food.
 • Avoid sugar substitutes.
 • Eat in moderation.
 • Drink plenty of water.
 • Eat lots of vegetables and fiber.
 • Minimize the amount of red meat consumed.
 • Eat fruits and vegetable from the color of the rainbow for the phytonutrients.
 • Eat fruits low in Glycemic Index.
 • Eat food low in fat.
 • Eat organic.
 • Avoid gluten in your food.
 • Eat healthy forms of protein.

Important Note: All our bodies have unique needs and sometimes what is true for many may not be true to you. Some things may not work for some due to variance in body type and medical issues involved. Before you embark in any dietary changes or exercise program, always consult your physician to make sure your diet or exercise program is not causing any issues on your medical well-being due to any underlying pathology you may have. Also, some diets are more appropriate for certain blood types. If you want more information, read *Eat Right 4 Your Body Type* by Dr. Peter J. D'Adamo. For example, type A blood type should eat more of a vegetarian diet. Type B should eat a more varied diet including meat. Other factors which may affect the appropriate nutrition include the particular genotype one has.

6. Get Help.
   • Clergyman or woman.
   • MFT/Counselor.
   • Physician.
   • Psychiatrist/Psychologist.
   • Hypnotherapist.
   • PSYCH-K Facilitator.
   • NeiGong Practitioner.
   • Spiritual Advisor or Guide/Life Coach.

7. Master Your Mind Universe.
   • Choose to be happy.
   • Choose to love what you do.
   • Imagine and visualize the life and day you want.
   • Release the belief about stress.
   • Be the creator of your mind universe.
   • Choose to smile until you feel better.
   • Align yourself with Divinity.
   • Choose to surround yourself with positive people.

8. Practice Deep Breathing.
   • Practice breathing in the nose 5-10 seconds bringing in positive energy.
   • Hold your breath for the same length of time.
   • Exhale through pursed lip same length of time and release all the negative energies.

- Do this for 1-5 minutes until symptoms dissipate.

9. Consult a Health Practitioner, Physician and Holistic Practitioner.
   - Discover which medications, supplements or homeopathic supplements may be helpful.
   - If you are seeing a medical physician and alternative health practitioner, make sure that both sides know what you are taking.

10. Join a Church or Spiritual Group.

11. Read Spiritual or Inspirational Books.
    • Dr. Wayne Dyer.
    • Joel Osteen.
    • Dr. Deepak Chopra.
    • Barbara Hay.
    • Paul Ferrini.
    • The Bible.
    • The Bhagavad Gita.
    • Tao Te ching.
    • Autobiography of a Yogi.

12. Pray.
    • Pray for yourself.
    • Pray for your family.
    • Pray for your friends.
    • Pray for those in need.
    • Pray for the world.

13. Forgive.
    - Forgive daily those who have hurt you and forgive yourself of wrong done to others.
    • Forgive, forget and release with no regrets.
    - A good thing to say to yourself is: <Name>, I forgive you. I love you. I'm sorry that this

happened. I pray that God blesses you and grants you peace, happiness, and love.

14. Give.
    • Give to the needy.
    • Donate to charitable organizations.
    • Be of service to your family.
    • Be of service to your friends.
    • Share your talents to the seniors and those who are ill including children.

15. Get a Pet.
    • Interact and play with your pet daily.
    • Experience the unconditional love that your feline or canine friend can offer.

16. Start a Hobby.
    • Learn a new language.
    • Learn a new skill.
    • Try a craft, art, or something new.

17. Minimize the News and TV.
    • Get unplugged.
    • Stay off the computer for a while.

18. Practice Gratitude.
    • Always be cognizant of all the blessings you have in life.
    • There is always someone who is worse off than you.
    • Count your blessings.

Nutrition for the Mind

I. Visual Nutrition.
    • Watch movies that inspire.
    • Read books that inspire.

- Spend time searching for Divinity in nature.
- Watch motivational speakers or programs live or on TV.
- Avoid things that make you anxious, degrade people or causes violence.
- Watch comedies.
- Visualize or imagine yourself as a better person.
- Avoid any imaginations or visualizations of yourself in any way negative.

II. Auditory Nutrition.
- Listen to music that is uplifting.
- Listen to classical music.
- Listen to inspirational music.
- Listen to the sound of water flowing from a waterfall, sound of the waves.
- Listen to the sounds of nature.
- Avoid listening to too much negativity.
- Avoid listening to gossip.
- Listen to motivational CDs.

CHAPTER 8

Reflection

When I think of San Francisco now, I think of it as a city of hope, joy, love and resilience. The city was destroyed by the great quake of 1906 mostly due to the widespread fire damage. The city emerged from the ashes and was reborn again as a robust city and became a haven for all groups of people who sought opportunities. In a way, I see my spiritual journey a little like San Francisco. My old self was destroyed and burned to the ground by all the metaphoric calamities I had inside of me. However, I also arose from the ashes to rebuild and reclaim my Divine self – like the Phoenix rising from the ashes – reborn.

We can all choose to focus on the negative or look at the good in every situation and learn from it. I now realize that I needed my parents, family, friends and all that has happened to me to help me become the person I am today. I have learned to have patience, gratitude, love, forgiveness and compassion for my parents. I came to realize how my parents were not bad parents or people after all. I realized they did their best to support us given the tools they had at their disposal. For many years, I had so much anger towards my parents and blamed them for all my shortcomings. That did me no good. It ultimately made me a prisoner to my parents and stunted my personal and spiritual growth.

I have learned that it is important to be mindful of what we say to one another especially those in authority positions like a parents, teachers, coaches, bosses, doctors, health care practitioners, martial arts instructors or masters, gurus, spiritual guides, etc. Words used correctly and positively can bring forth a future of happy children, adults, society and civilization. Conversely, words used in a negative disparaging way, produces unhappy and unkind children, adults, society and civilization full of conflicts and divisiveness. Remember to spread love in our thoughts, words and actions and trust in God for with him and his fullness of love, all things are possible. Many of us have abandoned ship and put our mind's universe on auto-pilot. That life never finds peace and true happiness. It is time to get back on the helm and reclaim your position as the commander of your mind universe and take actions and make a choice and decision to steer yourself towards the direction of your destiny.

When I was young, I remembered being told I am stupid by various people and it affected me profoundly and for so many years. Then in high school, I remember one teacher who told me that I wrote well. I didn't think much of it at the time because I had so much junk in my mind. However, he told me that only once but the words somehow survived the apocalyptic destructions that were done by years of negativity from all those around me. After many years of soul searching and healing, the idea that I could write well resurfaced and I embraced it.

We are human and make the mistakes of saying the wrong thing or doing the wrong thing. I am no exception. I have made many mistakes with my children and said many words I know are not Divine, spiritual or uplifting. On the contrary, I said words that hurt, cut and damaged their egos because I was not happy with what they were doing. However, what I have done (consciously) is to work hard on instilling in my children's minds that they are not stupid, dumb or whatever negative words I might have said. After things have settled down, I always go back to my children and tell them that I was wrong for what I said. I tell them I did not mean it and it was only through my inability to better express myself that I blurted out those negative words. I explain to them that I am not happy with their behavior and try to elucidate to them what they did wrong. After I do that, I can literally feel all the heaviness of the negative energy lift away and soon my children are back to normal again. So it is ok to make mistakes, just correct things as you go to avoid the gaping wounds we may create with our words.

We need to remember the power we have over our mind universe with our words, thoughts, and intentions. Unfortunately, we easily affect the mind universe of others by what we think, say and do. When that happens, we create a wave of negativity that starts from us and goes into the body of water or ocean of the person we are talking to or dealing with. I believe that our negativity with thoughts, intentions and words travels through our inner sea and may affect our organs, tissues, nerves, molecules, atoms, electrons, protons and neutrons. I believe that negativity suppresses the Divinity that is within us. When that happens, our body cannot be one with God and the universe. What ensues is chaos. When chaos goes on for too long, our immune system weakens and we become ill. That wave of negativity travels through us then to the person we are directing that energy towards.

The wave of negativity continues to the next person and so forth. In a day, perhaps one dozen or more people can be affected by the negative words and intention you generated. This vicious cycle will not stop until we become aware of ourselves and are vigilant with only saying words of kindness, gratitude, compassion and love. Saying words that edify and are positive will create a better world for us personally and eventually collectively. This concept is very important and must be practiced daily 24/7 for ourselves, our children and for the evolution of our civilization. We can all be a part of the movement to co-create a better tomorrow for all of us. Together with hope, love, kindness, compassion, love, forgiveness in our words, thoughts, intentions and actions, a whole new world can be born- a world devoid of negativity but full of love and prosperity. Let's dare to imagine this. It only takes a spark to get a fire going.

A friend of mine, Jacob, gave me a beautiful gift once. It was a decorative plaque that had two doors in front. It was made of metal and was gold in color. It had intricate leaf designs throughout. With the doors closed, it appears as a beautiful and ornate gate that leads to a special place like a temple, shrine or palace. At first glance I was happy to just have a beautiful wall display. However, I soon realized that there were two small handles on it so I gently pulled on it and it slowly opened it up. Inside the exquisite gates was a mirror. Most people will just look at it and not think much about it. However, I realize the profound message that was there instantly. All spiritual paths lead to our inner selves, where the truth and secrets of the universe are within. When one follows the spiritual path and meditates daily and becomes one with the Source, Divinity, or God, then the subtle truths begin to review themselves to us. And when they do, what mother always told me is true, "the truth shall set you free."

Incidentally, according to one source, "the leaf signifies The Truth." One of the meanings of the Gold color of the mirror display is, "Wisdom." In the spiritual path, nothing happens by chance. We are not alone and there is a Divine intelligence out there.

Searching for God within is the key to true happiness, love, and success. The road and path to reaching him only brings us to higher consciousness and higher spiritual evolution. Sometimes it can be confusing who is God and where he is? God has so many names and faces to all his people. In the Kabbalah, there are even 72 names of God that are powerful when said. God may look different in each culture but I truly believe there is only one God with many manifestations. Where is he is not the question but where is he not should be the question. God is omnipresent. Most of us look into the stars, sky, and universe when we think about God. What we don't realize is that he is closer than we think. He is within our bodies and minds. The universe is within and without. I recently looked at a photo of a proton and couldn't believe how it looked like a snapshot of the universe. God is within and without.

As we are born into this world, we forget that we all are a piece of the spark from our source. That spark of light is hidden in the gaps between our DNA. As we go from our macroscopic world to our microscopic world, we find out where the Divinity exists within us. As we go from cell, to molecules, to atoms, to electrons, to neutrons, to protons, and beyond that, we end up finding a field of energy and vibrations. That is where I believe is where our soul and God exists. I recently heard a quantum physicist talk about how at the sub-nuclear level we are connected to the collective consciousness or Divine intelligence.

When we meditate and clear our mind, we can reach that oneness with our source. It is that magic moment when the universe within and without become one. It is the moment we are in communion with Divinity. When we reach that oneness and live a truly spiritual life (with some help from a spiritual guide), the Divine realm opens and we no longer wonder if we are alone. We realize and know that we are all part of this beautiful and Divine universe. If we still our mind in the presence of Divinity, the subtle truth can manifest within and guide us toward manifesting the light within. The light within is part of the light without which is the light of God. His light is pure, divine and unconditional love. Living a life of gratitude and love only brings more light in our life to truly manifest the Divine being we truly are. Once we have surrendered to the process, we become beacons of light that brings love and hope to all those in darkness. It is that process which will uplift and transform humanity one person at a time. The process of finding God only leads to true happiness, love and self-realization. With the love of God, all things are possible.

CHAPTER 9

Inspirational Words

May these words, poems, quotes, prayers, and mantras support you in your own spiritual awakening as they have done for me.

Prayers

On the Wall of Mother Teresa's Home for Children in Calcutta (Excerpt)
"People are often unreasonable, irrational, and self-centered. Forgive them anyway."

Serenity Prayer
God grant me the Serenity to accept the things I cannot change. The Courage to change the things I can, and the Wisdom to know the Difference.
—Reinhold Niebuhr

Poems

Press On (excerpt)

"Persistence and determination alone are omnipotent."
—Calvin Coolidge, 30th President of the United States of America.

Love is...

Love is a gift to us from Divinity, planted in our heart and soul. It is meant to be shared, nourished and developed. Love is an act of giving unselfishly and unconditionally to those in need.

It is an emotion that transcends logic and human understanding. Love is eternal and can heal the wounds of the heart, mind and soul. Love is the essence of life and the antidote to civilization.

Love is total acceptance of self, others and others and works in harmony and attunement with the cosmic.

To truly live, one must be able to receive, give and share that love. Spread love, and not war and the world will be a better place...like the song says, "All we need is love."
— Blake Sinclair

Our Deepest Fear (excerpt)

"We are born to make manifest the glory of God that is within us."
—Marianne Williamson[10]

Reader's Favorite Quotes

"It is at the intersection of all religions and mysticisms that one truth exists."

"You find your purpose through alignment with the Divine."

"Meditation is the ultimate gateway to connecting with Divinity."

"Most people don't realize the power they have over their mind universe."

"Perseverance makes up for our flaws in life."

"Words can say much but our touch can show depth to our words and soul."

"Prayer is how we connect with one another through space and time."

"Spirituality is the path that liberates us from the delusions of the material world."

Mantras

Om Mani Padme Hum
   This mantra means:
   Om – Generosity,
   Ma – Ethics,
   Ni – Tolerance and patience,
   Päd – Perseverance,
   Me – Concentration,
   Hum – Wisdom.

Lokah Samastha Sukhino Bhavantu
   This mantra means:
   May peace and happiness prevail.[11]

Gyatri Mantra
   Aum

Bhuh Bhuvah Svah
Tat Savitur Varenyam
Bhargo Devasya Dheemahi
Dhiyo Yo nah Prachodayat

This mantra means:
Oh creator of the Universe!
We meditate upon they supreme splendor.
May thy radiant power
Illuminate our intellects,
Destroy our sins and guide us in the right direction.

CHAPTER 10

A Message for You

My Friend,

Begin the journey now and you will find the Divinity within. We are all special and unique people but when we let Divinity work with us and dwell within us, all things are possible and the extraordinary is possible and we learn that we are all Divine and special. Do not believe in ideas or beliefs that enslave you but, rather, believe in words or ideas that will set you and others free and allow you and others to soar and fly.

It is never too late to start the journey. Your life is already in transformation the moment you truly wish to change. All you have to do is decide now that you want to change and dare to imagine it. Choose to be a better person and follow some of the principles I have written and you are well on your way. God loves you and wants you to be the special person you were meant to be. Before I found myself I thought I was just an ordinary person. After I found my Divinity within myself, I realized that I am special and unique and have purpose and meaning in my life.

As Lao Tzu once said, "The journey of a thousand miles begins with a single step." My brothers and sisters, I wish you much love and success in your own personal journey to find true peace, happiness, and success in your life. May you manifest the Divinity within you and find true happiness, peace, and love.

God bless you as you dare to imagine a new reality for yourself- one full of love, joy, peace and happiness.

Namaste! Shanti! Shanti! Shantihi!
Love,
Blake Sinclair

ACKNOWLEDGEMENTS

I have so many people to thank but these are the people who have supported me in my journey:

To my wife,
Behind every loving, supportive wife is a man who is grateful. You have taught me so much about giving, loving, and selflessness. Because of this I have become a better father, friend, husband, and human being. You have given me every opportunity to grow and have supported me through each step in the process.

Although we have weathered some of the worst storms in life, we have committed to stay focused on accepting, understanding, and loving each other. Thank you so much for your support in my spiritual journey and willingness to being a part of it. Thank you for all the countless hours reading and proofreading my book. Your support and belief in my book is phenomenal. Thank you for not being mad at me when I woke you up in the wee hours of many mornings because I was inspired to write. You are truly an amazing wife and most importantly, an amazing friend. May the love that binds everything within the universe continue to nurture and radiate that spark of light within us until we can have fullness of the perfect Golden light of God. Your beauty radiates from within to without. Your beauty is within your heart, mind, speech, and action- that is true beauty. You are truly an inspiration to many people and especially to me. May we share the love and light of God to as many people as we can so that others may know that with love all things are possible.

To my children,
I want to thank you for bringing a new level of happiness and joy into my life. I am so honored to be your father. Both of you are evolving into wonderful, special, and loving young adults. You guys have taught me so much in life about patience, understanding, love and acceptance. I know both of you are destined for greatness! I am so proud of you guys and love you so much!

To my mother,
Thank you for the life you gave me. Thank you for allowing your love to emerge further and manifest itself especially during these last two years. Thank you for all the lessons you have taught me about life, living and being a better person. I have internalized all the good principles you have taught me and have become a better person because of it. I am so proud of the person you are transforming into. You have taught me that with love, acceptance and kindness, all things are possible. Mom, I love you!

To my father,
Thanks for all your support for me and my family all these years. Thanks for reaching out to me in the end and beyond your physical existence. Thank you for helping me to realize that life is a continuous process and that love is eternal. I am so proud of the transformation you have made in your final days and the connection we shared in your final moments. In the end, you showed me how it is never too late to transform into a person of greatness. I love you, dad.

To my grandmother,
Thank you for all your support, and unconditional love through my darkest days. You were my strength and my salvation. I don't know where I would be without you. I love you Po Po. May God bless you with an abundance of love. Though we are separated now, I look forward to the day we meet again in all your glory. You have my deepest gratitude and love.

To my brother and sister,
Thanks for the support throughout the years. Thank you for tolerating my silliness and crazy moments. Thanks for always being there when I really needed someone. I look forward to even more depth in our relationships throughout the years.

To Julie Y. and Susan A.,
Thank you all for all your support and countless hours in helping me bring this book to life. Your selflessness is a testament to the beautiful and wonderful person that you guys truly are. I am so fortunate have you all in my life. May God pour happiness, love and abundance onto your lives. Also, Susan thank for the many wonderful years we shared on stage. You were truly a delight to work with on and off stage.

To Umang,
Thank you for your support in my nutritional awakening and in Yoga. You are truly an inspirational teacher and have so much to offer. I am just so happy to have met you. Thank you for introducing me to an extraordinary person, Dana.

To Dana,
Thank you so much for all your hard work, commitment, and dedication to bringing my book into fruition. Thank you for believing in me and all the support, enthusiasm and

guidance you have given to me in writing this book. Thank you so much for the countless hours you put into this book beyond the call of duty. You are truly an inspiration person and a beautiful soul with so much to offer the world. May God continue to pour abundance, happiness and love to your life. You are truly an amazing writer, coach and editor. It was my honor working with you!

To Airi,
Thank you for patiently working with me to materialize my concept and design of the book cover into a reality. You are truly a talented, wonderful, and delightful person to work with. Thank you for sharing my vision in creating such a beautiful and profound book cover that manifests the magnitude of the story and message of the book.

To Averi,
You are truly a Divine and special friend. You exude love and compassion in all you do. I am thankful for all you have done for me especially your gentleness in nudging me on my journey to spiritual awakening. Thank you for your ongoing friendship and support. You are truly a person of greatness, substance, and depth.

To Amma,
Thank you for being the Divine being that you are. Thank you for living an exemplary life and making a huge impact on the world and especially on me. Thank you for being the beacon of light for so many living in darkness. Thank you for helping me to experience the Divine love of God through your darshan.

To my Heavenly Father, Divine Mother, and friend,
Thank you for the gift of life. Thank you for never leaving me throughout my journey—from living in darkness to seeing the light you give me, others, and all of creation. You have my greatest gratitude for inspiring me to write

this book of love and hope. It is from thy perfect love from whence all goodness comes. May this book transform all who read it as it has transformed me in writing it. Thank you for helping me to realize that it is the dance and balance between the darkness, light and our choice that create the beautiful, unique, and special people that we are. Thank you for showing me how in the midst of the muddy water of life, a lotus can thrive and bring forth the beauty of thy perfect love.

Thank you for helping me see the true beauty, jewel and treasure within the lotus. The beauty and profoundness exist within the sub atomic level of the lotus and all creation from the micro universe to the macro universe. It is there we see eternity and the beauty of thy perfect love that permeates all matters in thy beautiful and magnificent universe. Thank you for the gift of meditation, the ultimate key that connects our inner universe and the universe of thy kingdom. It is there where no duality exists but thy perfect love that connects all of us together. Lastly, I thank you as a humble servant for using me as an instrument of light and love to those who need it most. May we all awaken the light within and find true happiness, love and peace as we journey back towards the source of all goodness, love and perfection.

My Heavenly Father, how great art thou. With thee and thy perfect love all things are possible!

REFERENCES

1. Sathya Sai Baba Bibliography of Works: http://en.wikipedia.org/wiki/Bibliography_of_Sathya_Sai_Baba

2. *The Growing Popularity of Laughter Therapy,* (NPR Website, http://www.npr.org/templates/story/story.php?storyId=5165226, 20 January 2006).

3. Learner, Michael, *Choices in Healing,* (U.S.A, First MIT Press, 1996), 128–129.

4. Williams, Debra, *Scientific Research of Prayer: Can the Power of Prayer Be Proven?* (PLIM REPORT, Vol. 8 #4, 1999).

5. Ratzinger, Cardinal Joseph and Bovone, Alberto, *Joseph Cardinal Ratzinger's Letter on Christian Meditation,* (Buddhist-Christian Studies, Vol. 11, U.S.A., University of Hawai'i Press, 1991), 123–138.

6. *Effects of Mindfulness Meditation Training on Anticipatory Alpha Modulation in Primary Aomatosensory Cortex,* (Brain Research Bulletin, Volume 85, Issues 3–4, 30 May 2011), 96–103.

7. Stephens, Anastasia, *7 Health Benefits of Meditation,* (Food Matters TV Website, http://foodmatters.tv/articles-1/7-health-benefits-of-meditation)

8. Wathen, Grace, *Position of Hands & Fingers During Meditation*, (Livestrong Website, http://www.livestrong.com/article/508335-position-of-hands-fingers-during-meditation, 2 August 2011)

9. Branch, Solomon, *The Dangers of Fasting*, (Livestrong Website, http://www.livestrong.com/article/442148-the-dangers-of-fasting/, 14 May 2011)

10. http://skdesigns.com/internet/articles/quotes/williamson/our_deepest_fear/#note

11. http://archives.amritapuri.org/bharat/mantra/lokah.php

Audio CDs

Living in Favor, Abundance, and Joy
Joel Osteen
Simon and Shuster Audio
C2010 Lakewood Church
P2010 Simon and Schuster, Inc.

Good, Better, Blessed: Living with Purpose, Power, and Passion
Joel Osteen
Simon and Shuster Audio
C2010 Lakewood Church
P2010 Simon and Schuster, Inc.

How to Life Your True Divine Purpose: Making The Shift
Dr. Wayne W. Dyer
Hay House Audio
C P2010 Hay House, Inc.

Life After Death: The Burden of Proof
Deepak Chopra
Random House Audio
C2006 by Deepak Chopra
P2006 by Random House, Inc.

Eastern Meditation and Christian Contemplation Compared
Father Kevin Joyce, Ph.D.
Copyright 2008 Spirit Site
Recorded live at Theology on Tap on April 27, 2008.

Books

Les Miserables
Victor Hugo
Copyright 1987 Lee Fahnestock and Norman MacAfree
Signet Classics; Unabridged edition (March 3, 1987)

Tao Te Ching
Laozi
Copyright 1988 Stephen Mitchell
Harper & Row, HarperCollins Publishers

Hua Hu Ching: The Unknown Teachings of Lao Tzu
Lao Tzu
Copyright 1992 Brian Browne Walker
HarperCollins Publishers

The Bhagavad Gita
Translation by Eknath Easwaran
Copyright 1985, 2007 The Blue Mountain Center of Mediation

Autobiography of a Yogi
Copyright 1946 Paramahansa Yogananda
Copyright 1974 Self Realization Fellowship
Copyright 1981,1998, 2007 Self Realization Fellowship.
Thirteenth Edition, 1998. This printing, 2010.
Authorized by the International Publications Council of Self-Realization Fellowship

The Hidden Messages in Water

Masaru Emoto
Copyright 2004 Beyond Words Publishing
Beyond Words Publishing, Inc.

The Great Gatsby
F. Scott Fitzgerald
Copyright 1925 Charles Scribner's Sons
Scribner

Life after Life: The Investigation of a Phenomenon—
Survival of Bodily Death
Raymond Moody
Copyright 1975, 2001 Raymond A. Moody, Jr. M.D.
HarperCollins Publishers

The Power of Awareness
Neville Goddard
Copyright 2010 Pacific Publishing Studio
Pacific Publishing Studio

Spontaneous Healing: How to Discover and Embrace Your
Body's Natural Ability to Heal Itself
Andrew Weil
Copyright 1995 Andrew Weil, M.D.
The Random House Publishing Group

Eat Right 4 Your Body Type
Peter J. D'Adamo, Catherine Whitney
Copyright 1996 Hoop-a-Joop, LLC
G.P. Putnam's Sons

Websites

http://web.mit.edu/newsoffice/2011/meditation-0505.html
http://foodmatters.tv/articles-1/7-health-benefits-of-meditation

http://suite101.com/article/mantra-examples-for-meditation-a105014
http://archives.amritapuri.org/bharat/mantra/lokah.php
http://www.ammanewengland.org/blog/ammatour-boston-home/ammas-darshan
Amma.org
http://suite101.com/a/mantra-examples-for-meditation-a105014

Meditation Resources

1. Amma's organization that teaches the I am-Integrated Amrita meditation technique. www.amma.org

2. An organization founded by Paramahansa Yogananda that teaches Kriya Yoga Meditation. www.yogananda-srf.org

3. Father Kevin Joyce teaches Lectio Divina and the Jesus Prayer-method of meditation commonly practiced by Eastern Christians. All are welcome but the target populations are Catholics. www.stlucy-campbell.org

ABOUT THE AUTHOR

Blake Sinclair is a licensed occupational therapist, writer, and entrepreneur. He uses his diverse background, Western and Eastern techniques, connection to the Divine, and his 25 years in the rehabilitation healthcare industry to facilitate the healing process for his clients. He has dedicated his life to sharing the joy, love, and real happiness he has found with everyone he meets with the hope that they can experience it as well. He lives and works in the San Francisco Bay Area with his wife and two children. You can learn more about Blake and his work at www.dare2imagineit.org.

Made in the USA
Coppell, TX
17 September 2021